AF552773

STOP PRESS

India scores over Pakistan 2-1 in a historic Test series.

HOWZZAT!!

Kadambari Murali

Our flight left Islamabad 30 minutes late. No one cared. We had been on IC 012 for an hour and it had been an hour of happy chaos. The atmosphere on this special, unscheduled Indian Airlines flight that was going to ferry the victorious Indian team and all us reporters back to Delhi was carnival.

Everyone knew everyone else and everyone was happy and ready to party (and this had nothing to do with the Heineken cans being liberally distributed by an equally happy crew). Even the background music wasn't mournful for once – the instrumental soundtrack was of Kishore Kumar numbers like *Bhali Bhali si ek surat*, *Nadiya se dariya*, *Ye Shaam mastani* and the like.

Sourav opened a bottle of champagne, the captain of the flight opened another and we were off. It had been nearly a month-and-a-half in Pakistan and we were going home on a giddy high after India won its first-ever Test series across the border. It was also the first series win on foreign soil in over 10 years, the last being in Sri Lanka in 1993-94. Sourav had become India's most successful captain too and he rightly attributed his win to the players on his team. There is no doubt that this generation of Indian players is in a league of its own, as

Winners

One & All

compared to previous ones. They have a zip and a fight in them that hasn't been seen collectively in the past in Indian Test squads. This is not a team that depends on a couple of chosen individuals to take them home and that makes a huge difference. Someone, somewhere down the line has to perform but that someone could be anyone. And to a man, they all believe that if one person doesn't perform, another will. They have an aggressive attitude and a spirit that defies conventional notions of the timorous Indian player who lacks a killer instinct.

In this Test series itself, despite the 9-wicket loss of that second Test in Lahore, which many put down more to overconfidence than anything else, they pulled back superbly in the decider at Pindi. All of us watching the Indian batting crumble inexplicably at the Gaddafi Stadium, knew midway through the Test that the series was not about to finish here despite Yuvraj Singh's fighting century.

That century was the talking point of the next few days. It catapulted the talented Yuvraj into the running for a spot in the third Test despite Ganguly's return. Yuvraj, it may be recalled, had played in the first two Tests only because Sourav was out with an injured back. All the talk, those last couple of days of the Lahore Test (April 5-9) and in the days leading into Pindi (April 13-17), was about the opener's slot.

It had become painfully clear by then, despite no official announcement, that Aakash Chopra (who had not done anything much in Lahore) was about to be dropped so that Yuvraj could be accommodated on Sourav's return. This was clear even when Aakash walked out to bat in the second innings and the pressure on the young man, not even 10 Tests old, must have been tremendous. To top it all, he got a very bad decision from the umpire, adjudged lbw when TV replays indicated that the ball probably hit his bat first.

He was dropped from that final Test and there were protests from many sections of the media, who firmly believed that the opening combine, that was working quite superbly, should not have been tampered with. After all, forget his solid performances in Australia, Aakash had figured in that crucial 160-run opening stand with Sehwag in Multan, that was the foundation for India's mammoth score. But Skipper Sourav insisted that the change was only for this Test so that was that.

Multan Test highlights

- India (675/5 wickets declared) registered their highest innings total against Pakistan, surpassing their 539 for 9 at Chennai in 1960-61 and their third highest total in Test cricket.
- Sehwag (309 off 375 balls) became the first Indian to post a triple century, surpassing V.V.S.Laxman's 281 vs. Australia at Calcutta in 2000-01. He became the first batsman in the history of Test cricket to complete the triple century by

On Cloud Nine: Victorious Indian team on the flight back to Delhi

All the omens were good as April 13 dawned. Sourav, who had lost five tosses in a row to Inzamam-ul-Haq in the one-dayers (after which Rahul Dravid led in the first two Tests), won his first toss and put Pakistan in. On that surprisingly green wicket (it was a very sporting decision by Pakistan to go for a green top, India would probably have played safe in similar circumstances), the Indian pacemen – Pathan, Balaji and Nehra – struck early.

It was a very disciplined performance from India's pace trio, especially Balaji, who bowled a superb line and length to return his best-ever figures of 4-63 as Pakistan collapsed to 224 one hour before stumps on Day One. Only an unexpected ninth-wicket stand of 70 between Fazl-e-Akbar and Mohammed Sami saved them from total ignominy after being 137-8.

And when India batted, it was disaster at first glance. Even as people were discussing Sehwag's new opening partner – Parthiv Patel, as the team decided not to risk exposing

hitting a six. Sehwag reached his triple century off 364 balls – the second fastest triple century in terms of balls faced next only to Matthew Hayden who had completed his triple century off 362 balls.

- Virender Sehwag and Sachin Tendulkar, with their 336-run stand for the third wicket, set a new partnership record for India against Pakistan for any wicket. Sachin Tendulkar (194 not out off 348 balls) posted his highest score against Pakistan, surpassing his 136 at Chennai in 1998-99. It was his 33rd century and his 18th on foreign soil, equalling Sunil Gavaskar's record of 18 centuries overseas.

Lahore Test highlights

- Yuvraj Singh (112 off 129 balls) registered his maiden Test century, surpassing his previous best of 59 against Pakistan in the first Test at Multan.
- Sachin Tendulkar, with his dismissal on 2 against Pakistan at Lahore narrowly missed the feat of becoming the first batsman in the history of Test Cricket to aggregate 500 runs without being dismissed. However, his first dismissal in Test cricket this year took his average to 497 in three Tests.
- Inzamam-ul-Haq (118 not out) posted his 19th century – his first against India.

Heroes of the Test series: (from left) Skipper Ganguly, Golden Ball winner Kumble, Man of the Series, Sehwag, Man of the Match, 3rd & final Test, Dravid, with Tendulkar

Sourav or Yuvraj – India's 300 man got out to a first-ball duck.

But Sourav is a very lucky man. He stuck his neck out with the decision and Parthiv went on to make his career best score. His 69 was invaluable, as was the 129-run partnership with an indulgent Rahul.

Despite the loss of Sachin one run after Parthiv's dismissal, Rahul continued in his usual unruffled fashion. He batted through Wednesday and by the time he got out on Thursday – a final, tired reverse sweep off Imran Farhat that saw his off stump gone, he had spent twelve and a half hours at the crease.

He would probably have got to 300 if he hadn't been told to hurry. But the 270 he got was the cornerstone of the 600 India piled up and the third highest ever by an Indian. Dravid, incidentally, is the only player to figure in India's last seven Test wins abroad in the Ganguly era. And interestingly, the only time he has not had any role in the win was in the last win at Multan, when Ganguly sat out and he himself led the side.

When Pakistan came out to bat again, they had clearly already given up. They kept trying to get out, played like it was a one-day game while the Indians just sat back and laughed as they picked up the wickets.

Rawalpindi Test highlights

- Rahul Dravid (270 off 495 balls) posted his career best Test score, becoming the first Indian to post five double centuries in Test cricket.
- The Indian triumph by an innings and 131 runs is their biggest ever overseas win.
- After 24 years, India has won a Test series against Pakistan – their first win on Pakistani soil.
- With 15 wins under his captaincy, Ganguly became the most successful captain with this victory. He is the first Indian captain to have won a Test in 7 different countries.

Victory dance: India wins the Test series

Eventually, India won by an innings and 131 runs. History had been made. Befittingly, it was the captain of the team, Sourav, who took the last catch.

What followed was a wild dance around the pitch by the winning side. A standing ovation followed them off the field. With true sporting spirit, the Pakistanis joined in too – but also burst into their national anthem, and strains of *'Hum honge kamyaab ek din'*. It was a touching attempt to keep their spirits up, and it pulled at the heartstrings, more so when the camera focussed on Inzamam sitting in the balcony. The stoic expression on his face said it all. But then, all's fair in love and cricket.

In the dressing room, it was champagne time. As corks popped, it was obvious that our heroes did more than drink the bubbly – in their exuberance, they poured it on themselves, drenching themselves with the stuff.

For India, it was celebration all the way. After dinner at Hotspot, the hottest dining spot in Islamabad, some of the team members danced the night away at Bassment, the disco at the Marriot Hotel.

Then it was homeward bound – to a resounding heroes' welcome.

Cricketing Ties

Neighbours' Pride

Match referee Ranjan Madugalle prefers this large and heavy Jamaican five dollar coin for the toss. During the toss before a series in the West Indies, the coin landed in a crack in the pitch. The crack was odd enough but more interesting was that the coin landed in it, and stood on edge! It could not be determined whether it was head or tails, and the coin had to be tossed again.

Victory for India: Fifth and final One-day International, Lahore, March 24

SAHARA
BADANI
70

4

INDIA-PAKISTAN

Cricketing Ties

Neighbours' Pride

Photographs
Pradeep Mandhani

Statistics
Rajesh Kumar

Lustre Press
Roli Books

The Playing Fields of Cricket
Omar Kureishi
19
SAHARA
INDIA
SAMSUNG

An ecstatic Afridi gets Ganguly's wicket:
Fourth One-day International, Lahore, March 21

Sachin scores a century as Shoaib Akhtar applauds:
Second One-day International, Rawalpindi, March 16

SAHARA
SAMSUNG
SAMSUNG
SAMSUNG

India & Pakistan: A Long Innings

Ayaz Memon

34

Pak rejoices as Sami eliminates dangerous Sehwag:
Fourth One-day International, Lahore, March 21

More than Cricket

In Lahore: **Madhu Trehan**
Karachi & Beyond: **Nina Martyris**

Men in blue up in arms: India's appeal against Inzy denied,
Fourth One-day International, Lahore, March 21

DIGITAL
SAHARA
INDIA
SAMSUNG

क्या
आखिर
SHYAM

क्या पाकिस्तान
जगह
हैतोइन्सान!!
SUNIL MITTAL
S.K. MAHAJAN
ASSOCIATION

From Cream Flannels to Blue & Green

Sunil Warrier, Pradeep Vijaykar, Nitin Naik, Anant Gaundalkar

All's fair in love and cricket: Final One-day International, Lahore, March 24.

The Playing Fields of Cricket

Omar Kureishi

I write two weekly columns for *Dawn*, Pakistan's leading English-language newspaper. One is a cricket column and the other a political one. Thus, I straddle the fence between the sublime and the ridiculous. I have no difficulty in deciding which is which. But which cap should I wear in writing about the resumption of cricket relations between India and Pakistan? India's tour of Pakistan came with other confidence-building measures. It was a part of a process initiated by Atal Bihari Vajpayee, India's prime minister, and our president, General Pervez Musharraf. The respective cricket boards played no role in the decision-making. Cricket became one of the means of achieving political goals.

I am covering the present tour for a number of newspapers in Pakistan and abroad, including one in India. I have put on my cricket cap and kept my eye on the ball. When this tour is over we will know the cricket results. We will have to wait and see if there have been any enduring political gains. Certainly the cricket that has been played, has been played in an atmosphere of great cordiality and the welcome accorded to thousands of Indian visitors who came across the border or, from beyond the boundary, has been warm and friendly. The sight of the Indian tricolour and Pakistan's star and crescent, the flags of the two countries being waved to convey a common yearning for peace rather than chauvinistic belligerence ought to augur well, but will it last? There is a lot of history that must be expunged, a lot of hatred that must be detoxified.

Let me try and put Indo-Pakistan cricket in the context of my own association with it, not as a player or an official but as a spectator who sees more of the game, as a commentator and writer who has been close to the Pakistan team. For this, I need to provide some personal background of my romance with the game of cricket and how I got to be a cricket person.

'You mean that cricket commentator?' That's the way I am defined. It is not meant to be demeaning. It is often affectionate and can even be respectful. But it makes me one-dimensional. Luckily cricket is taken so seriously in the subcontinent, much more than a game, that a cricket person is declared something of a national treasure. The Pakistan government awarded me the Sitara-i-Imtiaz, a high civil honour but the citation made it perfectly clear that it was cricket-commentary specific. To hell with whatever else I may have achieved, it is to cricket that I owe my celebrity.

How did I get to be such a person? I have absolutely no idea, no more than I have an explanation why cricket of all games, should have taken the form of a secular religion in the subcontinent. Apart from being an expensive game, not only to play but watch, both in terms of money and time, it is not a simple game with its many nuances that gives it a mystique, the tea interval being only one of its sacred rituals.

This does not wholly explain why cricket has been my passion. If I was to be put under hypnosis, perhaps, some answers would be found. When Sir Edmund Hillary was asked why he had scaled Mount Everest, he replied, ' because it was there.' Cricket has been there all my life.

The first 'proper' cricket match I saw was at the Ferozeshah Kotla ground. Playing for the MCC was an Indian Maharaja, Bhupinder Singh, the flamboyant ruler of Patiala

The first 'proper' cricket match I saw was at the Feroze Shah Kotla ground. The MCC (Marylebone Cricket Club), with Douglas Jardine as captain, was touring India in 1933 and was playing against the Delhi & District Cricket Association. My eldest brother Nasir was playing for it and my father took me and two of our elder brothers, Humayun and Rafiushan, to see the match. We were seated in the Students' Enclosure. Nasir made 17 and was stumped by Lovett off Marriot but he hit a six and it was that six that made him my hero. But playing for the MCC was an Indian Maharaja, resplendent in his turban, Bhupinder Singh, the flamboyant ruler of Patiala and about him a local Schehrazade could have recited a thousand and one tales of Patiala nights.

The crowd at Feroze Shah Kotla took to him, but not in a kindly way. He presented a somewhat comic figure and every time he fielded a ball, he was hooted. Some of it was good-natured and some of it was not. There was a certain contempt for the maharajas and nawabs who were seen as toadies of our British rulers and their lifestyles were an affront to the millions of people who were mired in a desperate and measureless poverty. Though too young to understand the anger of nationalism, I remember the red-faced Tommies who came to our enclosure and warned us not to make fun of Patiala, or else. Or else what? The Tommies were hooted down. Thus, in a convoluted way, I saw cricket as a way of making a political statement, of beating the British at their own game and striking a blow for India's freedom. This sentiment has stayed with me and I must admit that even now it gives me greater pleasure when Pakistan wins against England than when it wins against India.

I had watched my first cricket match, men in cream flannels, wearing cricket caps and I was fired by an ambition that I too, one day, would raise my bat to a cheering crowd as I ran the neat single to reach a hundred. I was convinced of the secret strength of dreams.

During the tea interval, my father had us collected and we went to the pavilion. Sitting on a wicker chair was a young man with the smugness of a cat that had swallowed the canary. People were going up to him and shaking his hand and he was lapping up all the adoration. I too thrust out my hand and had my first handshake with a cricket star. I had no idea who he

Sitting on a wicker chair was Lala Amarnath, the first man to make a Test hundred for India against this very same Jardine's team. I could not have imagined that he would become a close friend and that he and I would broadcast together.

was until my father told me that he was Lala Amarnath, the first man to make a Test hundred for India against this very same Jardine's team. I could not have imagined that he would become a close friend and he and I would broadcast together. I never told him that he had been the first Test cricketer I had met, not to mention the most princely batsman India had ever produced. Lalaji did not need others to blow his trumpet. He was capable of doing so himself.

Lala Amarnath played a central role in setting the tone of the earlier Test matches played between the two countries. Pakistan was given Test status in 1952. It embarked on its inaugural tour in 1952-53 and it was to India. Lala Amarnath was India's captain. When India toured Pakistan in 1955, he was the team's manager. Abdul Hafeez Kardar was Pakistan's captain in both series. They had toured together with the Indian team to England in 1946. Both were headstrong and combative and it soon became clear that there was no love lost between them. They were fiercely patriotic and their mutual antagonism rubbed off on the players. Those were the days when it was assumed that the host country would be up to dirty tricks. There was a lot of tension though it must be said that cricket matches were not seen as proxy wars. This came later.

India's tour in 1955 was a special one for me. I made my debut as a cricket commentator. I was a working journalist then and minding my own business when Radio Pakistan asked me whether I would like to do the cricket commentary. Without hesitating for even a moment, I said that I would do it. I have always followed my gut instincts. I was not a stranger to broadcasting. I had done a fair amount when still a student at the University of Southern California and I had been told that I had a good microphone voice. I did the commentary and the listeners liked what they heard and I have kept rolling the dice like a gambler with a lucky streak.

Every cricket tour has its moments. Even a tour in which every Test match is drawn. It was a dull and boring series sustained by a bogus sort of rivalry. Except the Test match at Lahore and the memory endures for its poignancy. Maqsood Ahmed who was better known as Merry Max had come in when Pakistan was in a bit of a crisis The sun had been shining, not dazzling but with a winter softness so that the light had about it an evening shade. Maqsood always had the look of a man who was having a troubled lover's quarrel with the world. He was a professional cricketer and had asked for a fee for playing, prompting extra-patriotic cricket fans to write irate letters to newspapers. He had failed in the two preceding Test matches and irate patriots got even more irate calculating how many rupees each run had cost. He had much on his mind when he came into bat with Pakistan in a mini-crisis.

He had started watchfully, nothing merry about this Max. He played himself in, like a firework that crackles but does not burst into a star-spangled explosion. But as we say in cricket, he was middling the ball and his feet were moving. The self-doubts were falling off. His body-language became more assertive. Runs started to flow, he got into the nineties. The atmosphere at the ground turned electric and there was a buzz of anticipation. I was on the air and I milked the suspense, raising and lowering my voice to create an extra drama. When he got to 99, there was a pause and the field was rearranged to prevent a scrambled single. Finally, Subhash Gupte came in to bowl and Maqsood stepped forward, was beaten in the air and was stumped by Tamhane. The crowd was stunned, shock before grief. There was pin-drop silence before the buzz picked up again. A crestfallen Maqsood made his way back with heavy steps, stricken by some divine despair and a pall of gloom hung over the ground. The newspapers reported the next day that a listener had died of a heart attack in Bahawalpur.

There was also a private moment for me, moving in its way and which brought tears to my eyes, almost. One morning as I was getting ready to go to the ground, there was a knock on the door of my hotel room. I opened it and saw a *burqa*-clad lady. She unveiled herself. I did not recognize her immediately and she admonished me. She was Mumtaz Shanti, a heart-throb of Indian films, now a greying but still handsome lady. She had been a neighbour of ours when our family had lived in Shivaji Park in Mumbai. She had been married to Wali Saab, a film producer. She would return from filming with her pancake make-up still on and my brothers and I would be playing cricket in the backyard and sit and watch. I think we all had a crush on her but were of the age between boyhood and manhood, the treacherous netherland of transition. She became a great friend of my mother. She had brought a box of sweets for me and we talked, she asked about my mother, she asked about all members of my family. We were rolling back the years. Finally, she left, wished me well and the moment passed.

In 1991-92 Pakistan toured India. I was now working for Pakistan International Airlines and I covered only the Test matches, flying back to Karachi each time. I learnt from members of the team that it was a hard tour. The general reception was correct but not warm. The first was at Mumbai and this was like a homecoming for me. I had gone to school and college in Mumbai, played cricket on its maidans and left from there for California. I would return many years later but to another city and a different country.

I wondered if any of my boyhood friends were still around. But I was too caught up in the cricket to undertake a sentimental journey down memory lane. All India Radio invited me to be the guest commentator and allowed me to rub shoulders with the likes of C.K. Nayadu and the Maharajkumar of Vizianagram or Vizzy. C.K. Nayadu was my idol. He was our expert commentator, and had been a superstar – he was to Indian cricket what Sachin Tendulkar is now. Vizzy was something else. Love him or loathe him, he could not be ignored. He had fixed views and he had a battalion of admirers and an equal number of detractors. I got on well with him though we crossed swords in the Delhi Test match which Pakistan was on the verge of losing and a triumphant Vizzy kept repeating that the match 'is in our pocket.' I was on the air at the moment when Pakistan was able to save the match, and I said that 'obviously, there's a hole in Vizzy's pocket.' He was not at all offended and the next morning his majordomo arrived at my hotel with a parcel that contained two Benarasi saris and a Vizianagram tie that made me a member of an exclusive club. Lord Willingdon had worn that tie when he had been Viceroy of India. A charming note accompanied the gifts.

It was not a happy tour for the wounds of Partition had not healed. The tension one felt was communal rather than political. That is why the Kanpur and New Delhi crowds seemed more hostile and more agitated and the slogans they chanted were blood-curdling – in fact, in this context, the word 'chanted' is inappropriate. Calcutta and Madras were calmer.

I had not been to Madras though there was a family history. My father who was a doctor in the elite Indian Medical Service (IMS) was posted at Madras and two of my brothers and a sister had been born there. My mother had often talked about Madras. This Kashmiri lady had taken to heart what must have seemed a different country to her. Her smattering of English and her Urdu and Punjabi were worthless to her and she tried to learn Tamil without success.

The cricket tour may have been a disaster as far as cricket itself was concerned but the past kept creeping up and I would get reconnected. There was one private interlude that lifted me but I was merely a part of the scenery.

I was given a message that Mrs Swaminathan had called and wanted me to call back. Mrs Swaminathan had been a family friend, particularly close to my mother. She was a political leader but more a social worker. Her daughter Lakshmi had joined Subash Chandra Bose's Indian National Army and was 'the Rani of Jhansi'. I telephoned Mrs Swaminathan and she 'ordered' me to have lunch with her. I said that I would be busy with the Test match but would have lunch with her on the rest day. She said she would send her car to pick me up and so there was no escaping the lunch.

She lived in one of those splendid old bungalows. Splendid for the times in which it had been built, the British Raj, but home is what one makes of it and there was not a trace of opulence. We sat on wicker chairs, on the verandah, overlooking the garden with its magical row of flowers, dotted by tamarind and palm trees. Kites were gliding in the sky and an odd crow made an appearance, surveyed the setting and flew off. It was a quiet (and simple) family lunch, the only others present were Champak, the daughter of Pandit Santanam and her husband who was the Ruler or Chieftain of Burdwan. I had first met them when I had gone to Calcutta in 1944 and they had been friends of my brothers, Nasir and Sattoo. Champak was a beautiful woman, her beauty subdued rather than radiant. The years had been good to her for she was still a handsome woman, one or two silver threads in her black hair, now bobbed. She was draped in a pale green cotton sari and wore no make-up. She was thrilled to see me, as if I was a reminder of Nasir and Sattoo and other days. Her husband had gone to a public school in England and spoke in a clipped, *koi-hai*, accent and among those with similar accents, he would have been called 'a good chap.'

The lunch was merely an excuse for Mrs Swaminathan (I called her 'Aunty') to connect with my family and she carried out an audit, wanting to know about everybody, at the same time pointing out that I hadn't been born when my family lived in Madras. One by one, I gave her an account of who was doing what and who was where.

Mrs Swaminathan represented a time past, a system of values that had eroded. Her generation, not all of them, but a select number of them, seemed too civilized, too cultivated, too rich in heart, to be relevant in a world distinguished by crudeness and vulgarity and soulessness. This was a generation that had become strangers in the brave, new world they had fought so hard to establish. The values, the behaviour, the way of life they had hoped that they would pass on by way of a legacy had become worthless, anachronistic and *ye oldie*, a Gothic typeface. I accepted that the rules had changed but the rules should have incorporated what was good. Instead, it had shut it out. But Mrs Swaminathan was still sprightly, there still burnt a light in her dark brown eyes and she would still laugh, the laugh of hopeful years to come. When the time came to take my leave, she squeezed my hand with a firm grip and hugged me. I was glad she had been a friend of my family. I did not see her again. One must not overburden love.

Vizzy kept repeating that the match 'is in our pocket.' When Pakistan was able to save the match, I said 'obviously, there's a hole in Vizzy's pocket!'

But alas! The lights went out and cricket links were snapped not for the poor cricket that had been played but some political compulsion. Cricket ties resumed in 1978-79 and then snapped again and now resumed again. Is this what Arnold Toynbee meant by the rhythm of history? Rout, rally, rout, rally?

There is a revealing passage in Proust's *Swann's Way*, when the elder Swann, shattered and grief-stricken at the death of his wife, is persuaded to take a walk in the park. He is so overcome by the loveliness of the day, 'a charming day', and by the pretty trees, his hawthorns and his new pond, that he exclaims: `Ah! Whatever you may say, it's good to be alive all the same'. And then abruptly, the memory of his dead wife returns and he is perplexed, how he could have been carried away by an impulse of happiness. And though he could never be consoled for the loss of his wife, he would say: 'It's a funny thing now, I very often think of my poor wife, but I cannot think of her very much at any one time.' That's the way I look at Indo-Pakistan cricket. I cannot think of it very much at any one time.

Like father, like son?: A young Rajdeep (centre) with his father, ace cricketer Dilip Sardesai,(right) and Sanjay Manjrekar (left), son of the legendary Vijay Manjrekar. While Rajdeep captained his University team in Mumbai, Sanjay went on to international cricket himself

Icons Across Borders

Rajdeep Sardesai

The enduring magic of cricket perhaps lies in its ability to provide millions of adults a durable link with their childhood and teen years, a flood of nostalgia that can be reassuring and even romantic. In the year 1978, I was on a first-ever school trip to the Kashmir valley. Decades on, I perhaps only have fading memories of the photo shop in Pahalgam which had been patronized by Rajesh Khanna and Shammi Kapoor and of horse rides on the forested mountain slopes of Gulmarg. But amidst the blur, there is one sepia-tinted memory that has stayed with me: sitting in a restaurant by the Dal lake and watching my first ever Indo-Pak cricket match on a black and white television set.

Every evening we would watch the highlights package, and every evening we saw Zaheer Abbas carve apart India's famous spin quartet. The bespectacled batsman with a floppy hat never seemed to get out in that 1978 series. It was depressing, but cricket junkies have an enormous appetite for self-flagellation, and so the more Zaheer cut and drove the Indian bowling, the more we seemed to relish watching him bat. A few years ago, I met Zaheer and told him about how he had enchanted us with the sheer beauty of the cover drive. We asked him about that series. His answer was simple enough: 'I was in good form, and just enjoyed batting!' Sitting next to him was another legend, captain of the Indian team on that tour and Sardar of Spin, Bishen Singh Bedi. Large-hearted bowler and man, Bedi whose career was virtually ended by Zaheer's batsmanship, only guffawed: 'Why couldn't you have enjoyed batting against some other team!'

Zaheer was one of my original cricket heroes, a sorcerer with a cricket bat on the field, a gentle, smiling soul off it. (Eknath Solkar, the Indian all-rounder and easily the finest short-leg fielder of all time was incidentally the first hero). Proof of how fickle form and adulation is came only a year later when in 1979 Zaheer came to India. The general expectation was that

Javed Miandad

on the slow Indian wickets, Zaheer would once again butcher the Indian bowling. In the end, a young man from the cricketing never-never land of Haryana made Zaheer look like a novice. Kapil Dev, he with the thick moustache and even thicker smile, was ready to change the face of Indian cricket by giving it a fast bowling dimension. Then, at the peak of his powers, he had a remarkable series against Pakistan. His outswinger was like a curving snake, fast, accurate and always probing. Zaheer, genius though he was, fell into the pit, never to recover through that series.

I watched my first 'live' Indo-Pak match on the ground in that series. It was played in Mumbai. The city was then still known as Bombay, the Shiv Sena was around, but far away from the corridors of power, so there wasn't anyone who was going to dig a cricket pitch. Fans had lined up for days before the match to catch a glimpse of a game that had been billed as the 'revenge' encounter. Even Sena chief Bal Thackeray, we are told, watched the entire game over glasses of warm beer. This time, it was not Kapil, but Roger Binny, an enthusiastic and much underrated bowler, who did the trick of getting Zaheer out. Then, another old Mumbai hand, Karsan Ghavri delivered the knock-out blow in the second innings, and India were home and dry. The Pakistanis complained bitterly about the umpiring (nothing could have been as bad as what one saw in Pakistan in 1978), they even claimed that their injured star bowler Imran Khan had been 'seduced' by the charms of Bollywood. The excuses didn't really matter. India had defeated Pakistan, and none of us were complaining too much.

Ironically, in that moment of triumph for the Indian team, I discovered another Pakistani cricket hero. It is strange but while we all want our team to win, hero-worship can easily cross the Wagah border. And so, while Zaheer became yesterday's man, Javed Miandad took his place in my cricketing imagination. Now, you can't get two more different cricketers than Zaheer and Javed. One batted like an aristocrat with a lazy elegance, the sheer artistry of the strokeplay making batting seem like an opera recital. Javed, on the other hand, was the ultimate streetfighter, ugly to watch at times but hugely effective. Zaheer may have been the connoisseur's choice, but if you ever had to pick someone to bat for your life, then Javed, the man who learnt his cricket in the unforgiving gullies of Karachi, would be your man. He may not have even matriculated, but he had a sharper cricketing brain than any contemporary player, his on-field aggression a deliberate strategy that was designed to rattle the opponent.

For the average cricket fan, Miandad was the ultimate nemesis, someone who could assassinate with a cheeky smile and a bandit-like moustache.

In that Mumbai match in 1979, Javed scored a 50, then was given out to the left-arm spin of Dilip Doshi, and knocked the stumps in disgust. It was hardly the kind of behaviour to endear him to the Indian crowd, but it marked the beginning of a love-hate relationship that lasted over a decade. I followed Miandad's career with great delight, always happy when he scored runs, even though scores of them were made against India.

For the average cricket fan, Miandad was the ultimate nemesis, someone who could assassinate with a cheeky smile and a bandit-like moustache. In the 1980s, a Bollywood film had a villain named Javed Miandad, such was his ability to crawl under the skin of Indian cricket. The agony and the ecstasy of watching Miandad bat against India culminated in perhaps the single biggest shot in Indo-Pak cricket. It came in 1986 in Sharjah in an Indo-Pak one day international. One ball to go, Pakistan needing four runs to win. Chetan Sharma bowled a full-toss which Miandad smashed over mid-wicket for six. While one country jubilated, another went

Shoaib Akhtar

into mourning. For Miandad, the shot brought not just fame but money as well, a gleeful Pakistani supporter choosing to weigh him in gold. One man's fame is often another one's infamy. Last year, I asked Chetan Sharma about that ball. 'You know, I took a hat-trick in a World Cup match, but everyone asks me only about that one ball I bowled to Javed!' he said.

While one admired Miandad's spunky batting style (who can ever forget Javed waving a bat at Dennis Lillee on a cricket field), it took Indian cricket almost seventeen years to rid itself of the psychological scars of Sharjah. It happened in Johannesburg in another classic Indo-Pak encounter, this time at the 2003 World Cup. Unlike in 1978, when cricket was still primarily a sport, now it was an industry, with Indo-Pak cricket as its fastest selling item. Colour television, sponsorship, event management: this was now global entertainment, not just a cricket match. So, the build-up to the game was accompanied by incredible hype, especially surrounding the encounter between Sachin Tendulkar, the world's finest batsman and Shoaib Akhtar, the world's fastest bowler.

Not able to travel to South Africa, one watched the match at home on a big screen television, hired for the afternoon. When Pakistan scored 270-plus, there was a sense of uneasiness in the room. After all, with a bowling attack of Wasim, Waqar and Shoaib, it seemed that the Pakistanis were impregnable. One shot changed it all: Shoaib Akhtar of the flailing hair and bent arm, bowling a 150-mile per hour rocket at Sachin Tendulkar. The Mumbai champion who had grown from boy to man in cricketing terms even before reaching a voting age was unfazed. He simply hit an uppercut (there is no other way to describe the shot) that went sailing over the point boundary for six. Shoaib on bent knees was staggered, the Indian tricolor was waved excitedly, while we at home went ballistic. All through, Sachin looked impassive, a tribute to his singular focus on winning the match.

When India did win the match, it almost seemed as if we had lifted the World Cup. The sky over Delhi, and indeed the entire country, was glowing and crackling with fireworks. 'We did it, we beat the Pakis!' a friend shouted excitedly. The atmosphere was almost war-like, a bit like Colonel Vikram Batra on the foothills of Kargil blurting out his famous 'Dil Maange More!' line.

Sachin Tendulkar

Perhaps, it is precisely the crowd frenzy that accompanies an Indo-Pak cricket match that has led even liberal-minded voices to suggest that its best if the two countries avoid playing with each other. Some have even suggested that the two countries play only Test matches with each other since they offer the hope for an honourable, if boring draw, unlike a one-day match where the winner takes all. Moreover, in a surcharged atmosphere, one hardly needs to give more space to naked jingoism, and in some instances religious fervour masquerading as sport. I still remember hordes of young men on bikes waving flags after the World Cup victory and chanting *'Bharat Mata ki Jai'* in the national capital, even as there was tension in certain communally sensitive localities in Ahmedabad. Cricket hardly needs to become the pitch on which religious bigots are allowed to fashion their politics.

This is also a concern that has been expressed by some ahead of this Indo-Pak series. A section of the political establishment was keen not to hold the series before the general elections. It might affect the feel-good factor, indicated one government minister. What of the players' security, chimed in another. It required the statesmanship of prime minister Atal Bihari Vajpayee to silence the skeptics.

The problem of security may have been a genuine one, but it is a problem to be resolved by governments, not cricketers. Moreover, which jehadi would dare risk complete isolation for life by targeting a sportsman? (Remember how the LTTE actually called a cease-fire in Sri Lanka during the 1996 World Cup because they didn't want to lose public support). The concern over the feel-good factor is also based on more imaginary than real fears. If India is growing at 8 per cent, if public issues are over-subscribed in the matter of minutes, if 11

If every defeat is not to be seen as a national catastrophe, and every triumph as a matter of national honour, then we need to play each other more, not less often.

kilometres of road are being added every day, then why should anyone be worried about the result of a cricket match affecting the national mood?

Unfortunately, cricket nationalism has often been used in this country in the past as a substitute for genuine nation-building (in the Cold War era, the communist bloc also used Olympic sport as an exercise in nationalism). In the Indo-Pak context, the fact that the politicians and the diplomats were unable to melt the ice over the Siachen glacier and the Kashmir valley meant that cricket became both a weapon and a victim of the impasse. While the pseudo-nationalists of the Shiv Sena variety saw the game as an opportunity to engage in Pak-bashing, there were other woolly-headed liberals who actually believed that playing sport with each other would eventually become part of the conflict-resolution mechanisms. Every time Indo-Pak relations deteriorated, cricket became the first casualty. We didn't play cricket between 1961 and 1978, a period in which the two countries fought two wars with each other. We didn't play cricket for a period in the 90s because Pakistan was seen to be sponsoring cross-border terrorism in Kashmir. And we didn't want to play cricket after Kargil because how could you play sport with a country intent on seizing a piece of your prized real estate.

Caught in the crossfire are the players, who are expected to be perfect ambassadors one moment, then suddenly transform themselves into shrieking avengers on the cricket field the very next. One of the senior players remarked that before the World Cup match in 2003, the mood in the respective dressing rooms was akin to soldiers in a bunker, both sides desperate to emerge victorious in the end. 'We knew that even if we didn't win the World Cup, this was one match we had to win!' admitted a senior player.

This intense pressure is hardly the ideal atmosphere in which to play cricket. A sports writer aptly described it as 'war minus the shooting'. Ironically, the solution doesn't lie in limiting sporting contacts, but actually playing more sport with each other. If every defeat is not to be seen as a national catastrophe, and every triumph as a matter of national honour, then we need to play each other more, not less often. That's the only way for the maddening crowds on both sides to realize that every game is not the ultimate battle, that there will always be another dawn when scores can be evened. Every sport has its traditional derbies and rivalries: England versus Australia for the Ashes, Brazil versus Argentina on the football field, Russia versus the Americans at the Olympics. The memories built around these competitive encounters always hold a special place in the hearts and minds of all those who value the joy of sport. It would be a pity if generations of Indians and Pakistanis were denied the opportunity of watching a Shoaib-Sachin contest, or an Inzamam-Kumble face-off simply because the politicians can't get their act together.

My son Ishan is now nine, and for him this will be his first real experience of an Indo-Pak cricket series. I discovered my cricket heroes in that 1978 series. I hope Ishan too finds his icons.

India & Pakistan: A Long Innings

Ayaz Memon

My first ever cricket tour was to Pakistan, in 1982-83. I was in Delhi for the Asian Games, and rather than fly to Lahore, decided to walk across the Wagah border, which seemed like a lot more fun. At the checkpost, though, the immigration official looked bereft of any joy as he scoured my documents. 'Are you really here for cricket?,' he quizzed. I showed him my credentials as newspaperman. His stern face suddenly broke into a smile. 'Welcome to Pakistan,' he said. '`Whatever the differences, we both love cricket. But remember, this time we will beat you.'

I could have argued a case for the strong Indian team led by Sunil Gavaskar, but the mere fact of getting past immgration mitigated the response. What remained in memory was the opposing sentiments of cooperation and competition going hand-in-hand. There was the 'bhaichara,' and there was also the one-upmanship, which has not only made cricket between India and Pakistan unique, but in a wider context, defined the relations between the two countries. Needless to say, cricket has also always reflected the volatile nature of these relations.

Pak celebrates: Afridi removes Yuvraj, 2nd ODI Rawalpindi, March 16

For almost a decade after the first series in 1952, therefore, the scars and trauma of Partition appeared to spill over on to the field of play. Given the socio-political impact of the Great Divide of 1947, there were huge expectations from people on either side of the border vested in their respective teams. This translated into a `let's-not-lose-to-the-enemy' credo that oftentimes hampered the free play of cricketing skill, and sometimes turned into ugly confrontations between players from either side.

Drawn matches became the rule, results were the exception. Wickets were generally overprepared, which meant batsmen would rule, or they were underprepared once in a while which meant that batsmen would rue. Both sides trained for a stealth attack on the opponent, but this did not quite turn out to be advantageous to any one side, if the record books are any indication. If anything, the pressure and tension seemed to affect the players adversely.

Allegations and counter-allegations by rival captains pertaining to doctored wickets and the like were common. Sometimes, the tension between the teams or the players would reach flashpoint. Rajender Amarnath, in his biography on his father Lala Amarnath, relates how the the Lala – coach and manager of the Indian team on the 1955 tour to Pakistan – almost came to blows with Abdul Hafeez Kardar, the home team captain. In turn, Pakistanis will relate with equal vigour how Hanif Mohammed had his hand slashed by a blade by an overzealous Indian fan.

Sometimes the rivalry between the two teams, their players and supporters, would take a quirky twist. In Lala's aforementioned biography, the story is told of how a `lady of pleasure' from Lahore floored a senior Indian player with her charms. So besotted was this player that he would wave his handkerchief to her from the field, and even wanted to stay behind in Pakistan and marry her! The Indian management detected subterfuge in this seduction, and

Sachin's spectacular catch removes Inzy: 5th ODI Lahore, March 24

after days of pleading and cajoling, finally succeeded in making the senior pro see sense!

After 1961-62, cricket relations between the two countries went into decline in direct proportion to the political barometer. Two wars – in 1965 and 1971 – widened the barren time period to 1978, when the Janata Government with Atal Bihari Vajpayee (then foreign minister) worked out a détente of sorts. The 1978 series was as historic as the 2004 one, minus the accompanying hoopla that the media implosion of this century necessitates. The game of one-upmanship of course persisted, but both countries were now 30 years older, and that much more wiser and professional.

It was also a classic cricket contest, and while Pakistan were runaway winners, India was not disgraced. Outside of the narrow confines of heartburn that such contests inevitably create in some people, what emerged loudly was the presence of outstanding cricket talent on both sides that could play the game better than most – when they wanted to.

The 1978 series became the precursor for a see-saw cricket battle between the two countries for the next decade which showcased subcontinent skills, Oriental magic at its best. Look at the litany of high quality players during this period – Bishen Singh Bedi, Asif Iqbal, Mushtaq Mohammed, Sunil Gavaskar, Javed Miandad, Kapil Dev, Majid Khan, Dilip Vengsarakar, Gundappa Viswanath, Mohammed Azharuddin, Abdul Qadir, Sanjay Manjrekar, Wasim Akram, Waqar Younis, Sachin Tendulkar – to appreciate the contribution of the Indian subcontinent to the sport. Add to this what talent came earlier and later – Fazal Mahmood, Vinoo Mankad, Ghulam Ahmed, Imtiaz Ahmed, Hanif Mohammed, Polly Umrigar, Ramakant Desai, Nazar Mohammed, Nari Contractor et al in the 1952-1961 era and post-1989, Rahul Dravid, V.V.S. Laxman, Shoaib Akhtar, Inzamam-ul-Haq, Virender Sehwag, Yousuf Yohana, Anil Kumble and Irfan Pathan among others.

DELHI, 1952-53

India lost their nine wickets at 263 when Ghulam Ahmed and Hemu Adhikari put on 109 runs in 80 minutes for the tenth wicket. The said partnership remains India's only three-figure tenth-wicket stand in Tests.

LUCKNOW, 1952-53

Pakistan's first win in Test cricket by an innings and 43 runs came in their second Test match at the University Ground, Lucknow, which hosted their first ever Test on jute matting. Nazar Mohammad (124 not out) recorded Pakistan's first ever 100. He carried his bat through a completed innings and became the first batsman to be on the field for an entire Test match. This was the only Test played at this venue.

Fazal Mahmood's Test bowling figures of 12

Romanticists might argue of what might have been had there been no Great Divide. But the harsh ways of history dismiss this as puerile thinking. Yet, in the cricketing context, there is much to cherish in the conflict between the two countries, as the brief series details and individual performances given below testify, and none better than the event which I can never forget. It exemplifies the best of the India-Pak cricket conflict.

It was the last Test of the 1989-90 series. On a grassy wicket, Pakistan's fast bowlers had the Indian batsmen in some trouble. Sixteen-year-old Sachin Tendulkar was at the wicket, battling to lead his team to safety when Waqar Younis bowled a snorter that rose steeply from the wicket and bloodied Tendulkar's nose. Pakistan captain Imran Khan, ruthless on the field, did not show any signs of emotion as the young batsman reeled under the impact of the blow. Tendulkar steadied himself, and after brief first-aid attention, settled down to face the bat again.There was a hush around the stadium as Waqar steamed in to bowl, everybody waiting to see which way the duel would go. It was a fullish length delivery and Tendulkar pounced on to it, sending it crashing to the cover fence for four. The crowd broke into raputorus applause. One also detected a hint of acknowledgement from Imran Khan at mid-off. The contest was razor-sharp, the desire to beat the opponent all-pervasive, but there was still room for appreciating genius, and of cohabitation.

1952

Captains L. Amarnath and A.H. Kardar.
Summary: 5 Tests, India won the series 2-1

Highlights:

■ DELHI: This was clearly Vinoo Mankad's Test. He had figures of 8 for 52 and 5 for 79 which not only established him as one

Abdul Hafeez Kardar

of the premier all-rounders of his time, but also helped India to an emphatic win. Incidentally, Hanif Mohammed donned the wicket-keeping gloves for Pakistan, and at only 17 years and 300 days, showed the natural ability which was to make him one of the titans of cricket in the next two decades.

■ LUCKNOW: Pakistan struck back with a vengeance on the jute matting wicket on which Fazal Mahmood was virtually unplayable. With his ability to cut the ball either way, the fast-medium bowler had all the Indian batsmen on tenterhooks and finished with match figures of 12 for 94. Nazar Mohammad, father of Mudassar Nazar, batted with monumental patience in scoring Pakistan's first century, carrying his bat through. He also became the first player in cricket history to be on the field for an entire match.

■ MUMBAI: This Test became memorable for Vinoo Mankad completing the 'double' of 1000 runs and 100 wickets in his 23rd match which was the fastest till Ian Botham got to the landmark in 21 Tests. Hanif Mohammed took a giant step towards being recognized as the Little Master when he batted with immense concentration for six hours in Pakistan's second innings.

■ CHENNAI: In a rain-interrupted match, the highlight was a 104-run partnership for the last wicket between Zulfiqar Ahmed and Amir Elahi. There was bittersweet irony in this, because only a few years earlier, Elahi had played for India. Incidentally, no other last wicket pair has scored a century partnership against India since.

■ KOLKATA: Deepak Shodhan became the first player to score a hundred in his first Test innings for India. Lala Amarnath, his captain, had done this in his second innings, almost 20 years earlier. Interestingly, Kardar set India a victory target of 97 runs in 15 minutes! But by then the series had been wrapped up 2-1 by Amarnath so there was rejoicing nonetheless.

for 94 (5/52 + 7/42) are still the best for Pakistan against India and his second innings figures of 7 for 42 remained the best of his Test career.

LAHORE, 1954-55

Mian Bux, aged 47 years 284 days, became the second oldest player to make his Test debut, next only to England's James Southerton, who was 49 years 119 days old when he appeared in the very first Test of Australia vs. England at Melbourne in 1876-77.

PESHAWAR, 1954-55

In four days of the Test played at the Services Ground, only 638 runs could be made off 395.3 overs and the run rate declined to 1.61 per over.

KARACHI, 1954-55

India's first innings total of 145 is still their lowest in Pakistan.

DACCA, 1954-55

Pakistan's 158 in the second innings remains their lowest total in a home Test against India.

KANPUR, 1960-61

M.L. Jaisimha batted 500 minutes for his 99 run out, executing only five scoring strokes in the entire pre-lunch session on the third day.

MADRAS, 1960-61

Haseeb Ahsan (84-19-202-6) conceded over 200 runs in the Indian innings and became the third bowler to concede over 200 runs for Pakistan, joining Fazal Mahmood (85.2-20-247-2) and Khan Mohammad (54-5-259-0) suffering the fate against West Indies at Kingston in 1957-58.

DELHI, 1960-61

Mushtaq Mohammad (101) at 17 years 82 days was Test cricket's

1954-55

Captains M.H. Mankad and A.H. Kardar
Summary: All 5 Tests drawn

Highlights:

■ DACCA: The attritional tenor of the series was established in the first Test itself, with only 710 runs scored on the first four days from 387.3 overs. If the spectators did not doze off in sheer boredom, or pelt the players with rotten eggs, it was only because an India versus Pakistan Test was still a novelty, and not losing to the arch-rival still the most sacrosanct objective.

■ BAHAWALPUR: The action shifted from East to West Pakistan, and Hanif Mohammed served notice yet again of his enormous talent by notching up the first of his 12 Test hundreds. Big-made Polly Umrigar rolled his long fingers over the seam to get the ball to cut and swerve while picking up 6 for 74, but neither of these two impressive performances were good enough to force a result for either side.

■ LAHORE: Just to show that cricket still languished somewhat in the Victorian age and had not yet completely become a young man's pursuit, Mian Bux made his Test debut for Pakistan at age 47 years and 284 days, the second oldest in history! But even that could not prod the two sides to get more enterprising, and the third Test of the series petered out into another dull draw,

■ PESHAWAR: If anything the series slumped into more defensiveness with batsmen refusing to take any risks, and the scoring rate dwindling to a niggardly 1.61 per over. Polly Umrigar's 108 in the context was a brilliant effort, establishing his all-round credentials quite forcefully, but still not good enough to win a match. India were set to score 126 runs for a win in the final hour, which in the context of the series, was never likely.

■ KARACHI: To compound the we-don't-want-to-lose tactics by both teams, this Test was hit by a thunderstorm that knocked off four hours play on the third day, effectively ruining any chances of a result though India had been bowled out for their lowest total, 145. Pakistan's two stalwarts, Kardar and Fazal, reached personal landmarks – the former making his highest Test score of 93, and the latter reaching 50 Test wickets. But that was not good enough to break the series deadlock.

1960-61

Captains Nari Contractor and Fazal Mahmood
Summary: All 5 Tests drawn.

Highlights:

■ MUMBAI: A tense Test match, replete with fine performances, yet no result. Hanif and Saeed Ahmed sparkled with the bat in a 246-run second wicket partnership that had Mumbai agog. In the second innings, Hanif scored 63 to reach 2000 Test runs, and also become India's nemesis. India's top order struggled against the Pakistan pace attack, but a ninth wicket partnership of 149 between P.G. Joshi and Ramakant Desai showed that the team was not without resolve.

■ KANPUR: One more match where the pitch made the players look like somnambulists. A daily log of 175 runs revealed the placidity of the track and the apprehensive, safety first approach of the two sides. Imagine, India's first innings could only be completed just before lunch on the fifth day! For the record, M.L Jaisimha batted 500 minutes for his 99 and made only five scoring strokes in the entire pre-lunch session on the third day, watched only by those who were still awake.

■ KOLKATA: In a rain-hit match, a result again became impossible, though Pakistan dared to set India 268 runs to win in three hours. Given the tardy tenor of run-making in the series, this was never on.

■ CHENNAI: A flat track facilitated a glut of runs from both sides. India scored a whopping 539, which was their highest

youngest century-maker until 2001-02.

FAISALABAD, 1978-79

Pakistan's main textile centre, Faisalabad, formerly Lyallpur, provided Test Cricket with its 49th ground. The Iqbal Stadium was actually cricket's first-ever ground to be named after a national poet. With the Faisalabad Test, the series between the two countries resumed after more than 17 years. There was an 11 minute delay at the commencement of the fifth morning when the umpires - Khalid Aziz and Shakoor Rana, reacting to language used by Sunil Gavaskar when Mohinder Amarnath was warned for damaging the pitch in his follow through, refused to go out.

KARACHI, 1978-79

Javed Miandad (100 & 62 not out) hit the

winning run with seven balls to spare, enabling Pakistan to record their first series win (2-0) against India.

BANGALORE, 1979-80

Mudassar Nazar hit 126 and emulated his father, Nazar Mohammad, who had also recorded a century as an opening batsman in Pak-India Tests. They provided the second father/son combination after 'Dave' and 'Dudley' Nourse to score hundreds (South Africa vs. Australia Tests) between the two countries.

On the first day of the Test, a swarm of bees had invaded the stadium and play was halted for several minutes when all the players and both umpires threw themselves to the ground, face down with their hands over their ears.

DELHI, 1979-80

Dilip Doshi who was declared run out when

then, powered by centuries from Chandu Borde and Polly Umrigar. Pakistan responded with as much panache and purpose, Hanif and Imtiaz Ahmed scoring 162 for the first wicket to seal the authority of bat over ball in the match. Thereafter, a draw was inevitable.

■ DELHI: Twelve successive draws spread over three series revealed the play-safe nature of cricket contests between the two countries. For the record, Polly Umrigar hit another hundred and his fifth against Pakistan, while Mushtaq Mohhamed at 17 years and 82 days became the youngest player to hit a century in Tests. Leg spinner V.V. Kumar bowled Imtiaz Ahmed with his sixth ball in test cricket to inspire some hurrahs, but there was little else to commend either this Test or the series.

1978-79

Skippers B.S. Bedi and Mushtaq Mohammed
Summary: India and Pakistan resumed cricketing ties after 17 years. Pakistan won 2-0

Highlights:

■ FAISALABAD: The textile town, also known as the Manchester of the East, produced a run feast. Zaheer Abbas led the way with a magnificent double hundred and Gundappa Viswanath returned the compliment with a strokeful century for India. A notable addition to the Indian side was an ebullient 19-year-old all-rounder Kapil Dev, who forced Sadiq Mohammed to wear a helmet. The build-up to the Test had been prickly, with players from both sides unwilling to cede any ground and there was an 11-minute delay at the start of the fifth morning when umpires

Bishen Singh Bedi

Mushtaq Mohammed

refused to take the field claiming they had been abused by Sunil Gavaskar after Mohinder Amarnath was warned for running on to the wicket. The match ended in a tame draw, but before Gavaskar had claimed his only Test victim, Zaheer Abbas for 96!

■ LAHORE: The chain of 13 consecutive draws was finally broken when Pakistan won this Test in an enthralling run chase. Set to score 126 in a minimum of 100 minutes, they reached their target with 8.2 overs to spare. Zaheer Abbas, in scintillating form, hit another double hundred. Bishen Singh Bedi became India's most capped player and also claimed his 250th wicket, but these milestones were obscured by the defeat. An ecstatic President Zia-ul-Haq declared a national holiday in the wake of the win.

■ KARACHI: Pakistan's first series win against India came in another thrilling run chase. When Javed Miandad hit the winning runs, there were only seven deliveries remaining in the match! Gavaskar made hundreds in both innings, and became India's highest run-getter, but this was small consolation in the defeat. There was something to cheer, however, in Kapil Dev's 33-ball swashbuckling half-century which was a sign of things to come.

1979-80

Captains S.M. Gavaskar, Gundappa Viswanath and Asif Iqbal.
Summary: India won 6-Test series 2-0.

Highlights:

■ BANGALORE: Pakistan's first Test match on Indian soil for almost 19 years petered out into a dreary draw. Mudassar

he left his crease to complain about the shadow of a large tree which was on the pitch, was allowed to resume his innings after he had successfully entreated acting captain, Majid Khan to withdraw the appeal.

BOMBAY, 1979-80

After nine drawn Tests in a row in India between the two countries, India recorded their first win against Pakistan since November 1952.

CALCUTTA, 1979-80

Making his 25th appearance in a row since his Test debut, Kapil Dev captured his 100th wicket in the record time of 1 year 105 days, surpassing England's Ian Botham's feat of 2 years and 9 days. At 21 years 25 days, he was the youngest bowler to claim 100 Test wickets, surpassing Australia's Graham McKenzie's record. Kapil, two days later, became the youngest to aggregate 1,000 Test runs, surpassing Javed Miandad's record and to complete the Test double.

KARACHI, 1982-83

Kapil Dev's first innings score of 73 was made off just 54 balls and included 12 fours and a six. He reached 50 off just 30 deliveries, which is the fastest on record for India in terms of balls received. Kapil Dev's figures were the best of his career at that time - 8 for 85. His figures included three wickets with his last five balls.

FAISALABAD, 1982-83

Zaheer Abbas, with 215 at Lahore, 186 at Karachi and 168 at Faisalabad, became the first Pakistan batsman to post centuries in three successive innings.

Imran Khan, with 11

Nazar plodded along for 340 minutes to score a century, and the big excitement on the first day came when the players and both umpires threw themselves to the ground, their faces down with their hands on ears after a swarm of bees had taken over the playing area for several minutes.

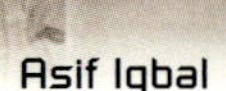

Asif Iqbal

■ DELHI: Another draw, but a dramatic Test nonetheless. Chasing a large target (390), India's batsmen showed heart and vigour and were only 26 runs short when the match was called off with one mandatory over remaining. The heroes were Sikander Bakht for Pakistan who claimed 11 wickets in the match, and Dilip Vengsarkar for India, who scored an unbeaten 146 in the run chase.

■ MUMBAI: Riding the momentum gained at Delhi, India got the better of Pakistan on a wicket that became a dust-bowl as the match wore on, winning in four days. It was a low-scoring game in which the Indian spinners dominated. Pakistan's star-studded top order, apart from Miandad and Wasim Akram, failed to come to terms with the track.

■ KANPUR: Pakistan had India on the hop bowling them out for a paltry 162 on a grassy wicket, Bakht and Qazi Ehteshamuddin doing the damage. But the track eased out into a featherbed after a while, the batsmen came into their own and the bowlers faded out. The match was a draw without drama.

■ CHENNAI: Revenge was sweet for India as they sealed a series win here in striking style. The heroes in this win were India's two premier cricketers – Sunil Gavaskar and Kapil Dev. Gavaskar's 23rd hundred drew out the venom from the Pakistan attack in spite of some splendid bowling from Imran Khan. Kapil Dev then upstaged the Pakistan all-rounder completely, smashing 84 off 98 balls, and taking 10 wickets in the match.

■ KOLKATA: The progress of the series had defined the fate of the respective captains. Gavaskar, riding a high, chose not to lead here since he had already pulled out of the West Indies tour which was to follow. The defeated Asif Iqbal announced that this would be his last Test. The match was doomed to a draw on a placid wicket, but Kapil Dev had the statisticians in good cheer, claiming his 100th wicket and scoring his 1,000th run in his 25th Test to become the youngest player to the Double.

1982-83

Captains Sunil Gavaskar and Imran Khan

Summary: 6 Matches. Pakistan won 3-0

Highlights:

■ LAHORE: The series opener was a high-scoring affair, though there were some portents of things to come when India lost quick wickets to Imran Khan. Zaheer Abbas, always a thorn in India's flesh, made yet another hundred, which also happened to be his 100th first class hundred. Sunil Gavaskar turned the spotlight on himself by completing 7000 runs, but the most entertaining phase of the game came when he smashed 68 runs off 56 balls, including 44,6420 in one over from Jalaluddin.

■ KARACHI: The high scoring draw at Lahore proved to be the lull before the storm. On a freshly laid wicket, Pakistan's bowlers, led by their redoubtable captain who got late swing at express pace, proved more than a handful for the batsmen. Zaheer Abbas made runs again, predictably, but the man of the moment (and the match) was Imran, who finished the game by taking five wickets for three runs in a sensational 25-ball spell.

■ FAISALABAD: There was a deluge of runs and hundreds for Pakistan,

Sunil Gavaskar

wickets (6/98 + 5/82) for the second Test running, emulated Ian Botham by scoring a century and taking 10 wickets in the same Test. His magnificent knock of 117 off 121 balls included five sixes and ten fours. In one Kapil Dev over he had hit 21-640461. Imran Khan, with 40 wickets + 247 runs, accomplished an extraordinary double. He is the only one from Pakistan to claim 40 wickets (ave.13.95 - strike rate of 33.48) in a series.

BANGALORE, 1983-84

No balls and wides were debited to bowlers' analyses for the first time in this Test match.

After 27 minutes of confusion concerning regulations governing the number of overs to be bowled on the fifth and final day, during which time the Pakistan team left the field, Gavaskar (87) was allowed to continue his innings. He duly completed his 28th Test century off the first ball of the last of the mandatory 20 overs.

JULLUNDUR, 1983-84

Anshuman Gaekwad (201) registered India's first double century against Pakistan, which took him 652 minutes (426 balls) and was then the slowest in all first-class cricket, obliterating Mansur Ali Khan, Pataudi's 622 minutes' display in the Duleep Trophy for South Zone against West Zone at Bombay in 1967-68. Gaekwad overall batted for 671 minutes, faced 436 balls and hit 17 fours.

Kapil Dev had dismissed Mohsin Khan with the first ball of the match.

Imran Khan

and more trouble for India. Four from the home team got centuries, including a third successive one for the indefatigable Zaheer, and Gavaskar carried his bat through as his side hurtled to defeat. But the most significant player of the match was once again Imran Khan, who topped a century with 11 wickets in a superb all-round show.

■ HYDERABAD: With a hat-trick of wins Pakistan clinched the rubber at this venue in roaring style. Batting first, Pakistan lost two wickets in two balls before Mudassar Nazar (231) and Javed Miandad (280 not out) got together to add a world record of 451 runs. There was a sense of deja vu in India's batting which collapsed once again to Imran's in-dippers. He claimed 5 for 8 runs in 23 balls in the first innings, and the die had been cast.

■ LAHORE: Like father like son. Mudassar Nazar emulated dad Nazar Mohammed in carrying his bat as Pakistan's much vaunted batting struggled against Kapil Dev who claimed 8 for 85 in overcast conditions. For the first time in the series, the Indians looked like matching Pakistan, but rain took over on the last two days, and the game was consigned to a draw.

■ KARACHI: Back in the coastal city, India's batting this time weathered the Imran storm capably. Ravi Shastri, asked to open, reached his maiden century to signal the resistance, and thereafter the match became a feast for statisticians. Imran added incrementally to take his tally of wickets to a whopping 40.

1983-84

Captains Kapil Dev and Zaheer Abbas
Summary: 3 Tests, all drawn.

Highlights:

■ BANGALORE: There was an interesting amendment to some old cricket rules, in that wides and no-balls were debited to bowlers now. But that did not seem to affect the soporific nature of the contest on a placid wicket, and where inclement weather took away more than 7 hours of play. For the record, Miandad failed yet again to make a hundred in India, this time being dismissed for 99. Gavaskar, however, was not to be denied his 28th hundred, though this came in some controversy with the Pakistan team being forced to bowl the mandatory overs to facilitate this landmark.

■ JULLUNDER: Rain followed the Pakistanis from the south of India to the north. The third day's play was washed out, and after Zaheer Abbas refused to make up for this by playing on the rest day, a draw was inevitable. Given the docile nature of the wicket, Kapil Dev's first ball dismissal of Mohsin Khan was a rare good moment for bowlers before the batsmen took over. Anshuman Gaekwad was a major beneficiary, scoring 201, while Wasim Raja made a century to ensure that Pakistan were not embarrassed.

■ NAGPUR: There was a lot of melodrama, but no result. Sandeep Patil, not originally in the team, was flown by a chartered aircraft to replace Mohinder Amarnath who was down with fever. Patil arrived after the first day's play, but could not contribute much in India's bid for a win. With three dull and dreary draws, India and Pakistan appeared to be back at square one.

Javed Miandad

NAGPUR, 1983-84

The Test match had to commence with one of its participants 600 miles away in Bombay. Due to fever, Mohinder Amarnath had to withdraw shortly before the start. As a result Sandip Patil, not in the squad of 14, was summoned by a special chartered flight. Patil actually arrived after the first day's play (October 5, 1983) had ended.

FAISALABAD, 1984-85

Mudassar - 199 off 408 balls in 552 minutes - became the first batsman to be dismissed for 199 in Tests.

Qasim Omar played the longest Test innings in Pakistan - 210 in 685 minutes (442 balls). His stand of 250 with Mudassar Nazar remains Pakistan's record for the second wicket against India.

1986-87

Captains Kapil Dev and Imran Khan

Summary: Pakistan won 5-Test series 1-0

Highlights:

■ CHENNAI: The tour got off with a run spree by both sides. Pakistan notched up a huge first innings total, propelled by Imran Khan's third century. The Pakistan captain proved less impressive with the ball, and India's response was equally emphatic. Krish Srikkanth raced to a hundred off just 118 deliveries with some audacious strokeplay and by the time the Indian innings ended, so had the prospects of a result in the match.

■ KOLKATA: The battle shifted from south to east, and while this match too ended in a draw, it was never short of excitement. India were minus Gavaskar, who had refused to play at the Eden because the crowds had abused him earlier, but the batting did not lack solidity or flair, with Azharuddin making a stroke of hundred. The match went back and forth, and in the last innings, Pakistan were set 356 to win in 285 minutes plus 20 overs on a wearing track. But Javed Miandad and Salim Yousuf held on grimly for a draw after the top order had been creamed off.

■ JAIPUR: Among the many highlights in the game, none was more significant perhaps than the visit of President Zia-ul-Haq in a `cricket for peace' mission, so reminiscent of the mood in 2004. He watched part of the second day of the Test, by which time Shastri and Azharuddin had completed their hundreds to take India to a good total after the setback of Gavaskar's first ball dismissal. But there was never any chance of a result.

■ AHMEDABAD: A fourth successive draw could not dilute the excitement of Gavaskar crossing the 10,000-run milestone. This came in his 124th Test, capping an outstanding career. A crowd invasion stopped play for 20 minutes, but after play resumed, it became clear that Gavaskar's landmark apart,

CALCUTTA, 1986-87

Sunil Gavaskar's sequence of 106 consecutive Tests was broken when he refused to play at Eden Gardens because of the crowd's abuse in earlier games. Sunil Gavaskar, for the third time in his Test career, was dismissed by the first ball of the match, bowled by Imran Khan.

JAIPUR, 1986-87

Pakistan's President General Zia-ul-Haq, witnessed a few hours' play on the second day as part of his 'Cricket for Peace' mission.

AHMEDABAD, 1986-87

Sunil Gavaskar, when on 58, became the first batsman to aggregate 10,000 runs in Test cricket. The invasion by a jubilant crowd delayed the play for more than 20 minutes.

there was no further merit to be dervived from the match. Ijaz Faqih made a hundred to underscore his utility as an all-rounder, but the series remained deadlocked.

■ BANGALORE: Pakistan made history by beating India in their own backyard. In a see-saw, low-scoring match on a dustbowl of a wicket, India paid the price for overconfidence after dismissing Pakistan for a low total. Instead of playing patiently to grab a big first innings lead, India's batsmen threw their wickets allowing Pakistan to crawl back into the match. In the final innings, India had to score 221 runs for a win, but the wicket was at its most spiteful, and it was only the technical brilliance of Sunil Gavaskar which brought his side within 16 runs of the target. In his last Test innings, the Little Master made 97, bowing out in a blaze of glory, but sadly for a losing cause.

1989-90

Captains Imran Khan and Krish Srikkanth. Summary: 4-test series, all matches drawn.

Highlights:

■ KARACHI: With neutral umpires officiating at both ends, this series got off with fanfare and high expectations, none greater than from the precocious Sachin Tendulkar who, at 16 years and 205 days, became the third youngest cricketer after Mushtaq Mohammed and Aqib Javed of Pakistan to play a Test. Though Tendulkar did not score too many runs, the Test will be remembered for statistical milestones. Kapil Dev in his 100th Test claimed

Kapil Dev

BANGALORE, 1986-87

Sunil Gavaskar, in his last Test match, played an excellent innings. With India needing 221 on a turning pitch, he played a superb innings of 96, lasting 323 minutes, during which he completed 2,000 runs against Pakistan, in the Indian total of 204. At the time of his retirement, he held the following world Test records: Most Tests (125); Most Tests in a row (106), Most innings (214), Most runs (10,122), Most centuries (34), Most fifty-plus scores (79) and most century partnerships (58).

KARACHI, 1989-90

For the first time in the history of Test cricket, two independent umpires - J.H. Hampshire and J.W. Holder, both from England, officiated in a Test.

Sachin Tendulkar, at 16 years 205 days, became the third youngest Test cricketer after Mushtaq Mohammed and Aqib Javed of Pakistan.

FAISALABAD, 1989-90

In India's first innings of 288, Pakistan's bowlers established a Test record by bowling 15 wides. (Zimbabwe surpassed this record by conceding 16 in England's first innings of 374 at Nottingham in 2000)

MADRAS, 1998-99

This Test was the first between the two countries for nine years and their first in India since 1986-87. This Test was to be played at Ferozeshah Kotla but was shifted to Chidambaram Stadium after Hindu extremists had vandalized the pitch. The Test won by Pakistan by 12 runs, produced the

his 350th wicket, and Mohammed Azharuddin, who only played the game because Raman Lamba injured himself at the eleventh hour, claimed a world record 5 catches in an innings. The best batting in the Test came from Sanjay Manjrekar who held the Indian innings together.

■ FAISALABAD: Another dull draw as the wicket played flat and true, reducing the bowlers to tears. India had another young debutant in fast bowler Vivek Razdan, but the spotlight was on the batting, with Azharuddin making a hundred and Tendulkar scoring his maiden half-century.

■ LAHORE: Javed Miandad, ever a man for the big occasion, scored a hundred in his 100th Test match. He had also scored a hundred on debut at the same ground. This turned out to be another tall-scoring match, with Sanjay Manjrekar stealing some of Miandad's thunder while making a magnificent 218.

■ SIALKOT: Imran Khan's frustration reached boiling point when Pakistan failed to win this Test too, and the series was drawn 0-0. If anything, India earned some brownie points by taking the first innings lead. Imran himself reached 350 Test wickets to underscore his greatness as an all-rounder, but the plaudits accrued to Navjot Sidhu, who made a fine hundred, Tendulkar, who made a fighting half-century and Razdan who took a 5-wicket haul on a dull surface.

1998-99

Captains M. Azharuddin and Wasim Akram

Summary: 2-Test series 1-1

Higlights:

■ CHENNAI: A riveting Test which Pakistan won by a a slim 12-run margin in spite of a throbbing 136

K. Srikkanth

Mohammed Azharuddin

by Sachin Tendulkar. The Little Master appeared to have the match under control, but skied Saqlain to mid-off with only 17 runs needed, and the tail collapsed like a pack of cards. The match had been shifted from Delhi following threats of violence in the capital, but Chennai, with a standing ovation for the victorious team, demonstrated why it is referred to as the soul of cricket in India.

■ DELHI: India struck back strongly to win this and drew the series. Their hero was Anil Kumble, who equalled a 43-year-old record when he took all hundred wickets in Pakistan's second innings. It was a wicket on which bowlers got assistance, but all things considered, this was still a tour de force.

closest finish to date in any Test match on the subcontinent.

Venkatesh Prasad produced his best bowling figures - 10.2-5-33-6, including a spell of 5 wickets without conceding a run in 18 balls.

DELHI, 1998-99

Anil Kumble (26.3-9-74-10) became the second bowler after England's Jim Laker to claim all 10 wickets in a Test innings. Thanks to his 14 wickets in the Test, India won the Test by 212 runs - their first win against Pakistan since 1979-80.

More than Cricket:
In Lahore

Madhu Trehan

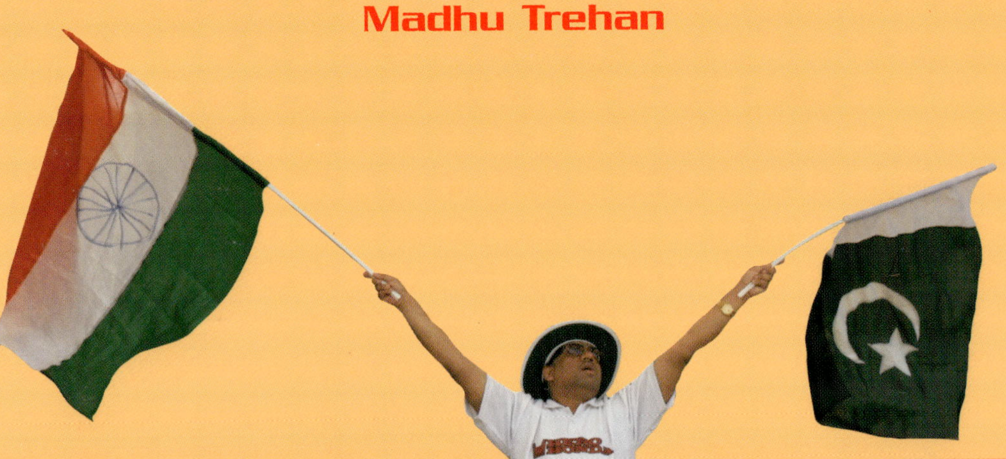

The future arrives of its own accord; progress does not.
— *Poul Henningsen, Danish designer and social critic*

The atmosphere is tense. India is winning the match. Indian spectators are screaming in euphoric support. The Pakistanis' silence can be cut with a knife. A Pakistani asks for my nine-foot Indian flag. I am apprehensive. Is he going to burn it, use it for a tablecloth or worse, hang it in his bathroom? He grabs it and runs around the stalls with three friends, waving it high, shouting 'Hindustan Zindabad'. One of them places a Pakistan cricket team hat on my head in fair exchange. A Pakistani seated behind me gives me bottled water when I throw a tantrum about no water to drink, no food to eat, the unbearable heat and unusable co-ed bathrooms. They offer us food. Hotelier Lalit Suri has brought a planeload of his large family. His children are remarkable in that they do not smoke, drink or spend time at discos. But that does not mean they are not spirited. One of his daughters vociferously tells off a Pakistani who happens to be wearing a T-shirt that says, 'I like to kick ass, especially when it is Indian ass'. When another Pakistani protests at her shouting, she explains the reason to him. He then changes tactics and joins her in yelling at his countryman for wearing such an inappropriate shirt. Lalit Suri magically materializes with mouthwatering stuffed parathas.

When we start winning the match, one of the Pakistianis says to me, 'Match *jeet lo, par dil dey doh*' (Win the match, but lose your heart). He repeats it twice, smiling, happy that we

Win the match but lose your heart

have made friends with each other. A Pakistani jumps to his feet while Rahul Dravid is batting and applauds wildly. My husband does not get up and his view is blocked by all the standing applauders. The Pakistani then turns to my husband and asks him why he is not cheering. My heat-exhausted husband answers, 'I thought since you are cheering, he must be out.' The Pakistani answers, 'No! He has hit a boundary and I am cheering for you!'

I have been christened 'Matchiss Aunty' since I happen to be the only smoker who was able to smuggle a matchbox through security. Shouts of, 'Matchiss Aunty, *matchiss doh*,' (Matchbox Aunty, give me a match) become as regular as 'Pakistan Hoo Haa Hoo Haa Hoo Haa!' A Sikh gentleman with his beard painted and dressed in all the colours of our flag and a Pakistani gentleman flamboyantly dressed in Pakistani colours dance continuously in front of the spectators with their arms around each other.

The natural sweetness of their language is of great advantage to them. Even a paanwala sells his paan, with, *'Yahan koi paan ka shuakeen hai ke nahin?'* (Any paan lovers here or not?) You feel embarrassed to admit that you are not *shaukeen.* The Indian crowd gorges on all the paan they can stuff. Listening to the distinct Lahori accent, it reminds us of our older relatives' style of speaking. Is it any wonder that once when I took my 90-year old father for a walk to Lodhi Gardens, he came back and told my mother he had gone for a walk to Lawrence Garden (Lahore). And then they both fell down laughing at his mistake.

The Delhi High Court Bar Association had a Friendship banner with both the flags and the lawyers were chanting for India. When it became clear that India was winning the match and the Pakistanis started to leave to avoid the rush, a young lawyer, Shyam Sharma, led the Indian contingent in singing, *Abhi na jaoh chodh kar, dil abhi bhara nahin* (Don't leave yet, the heart is not fulfilled). The departing Pakistanis laughed and waved. The lawyers had a great repertoire of Bollywood songs, appropriate for any situation, which were all familiar to the Pakistanis. There was a young Pakistani boy, around twelve years old, who refused to turn and talk to us while his older brother had become quite friendly. He was an angry young man. Angry with his team and angry with the Indians for winning. Only businessman Hari Bhartia succeeded in getting the boy to smile and shake hands.

By some coincidence, the rows in the stands we were seated in alternated with Indian and Pakistani spectators. It had been a rather polite and sober beginning, which meant applauding

United colours of cricket.

quietly and passing remarks in low voices so as not to offend. As the match progressed, so did the camaraderie. A commonality developed with the feeling that we were all stuck in the same boat. Both Indian and Pakistani armchair cricketers started sharing opinions, which then developed to sharing feelings. It was agreed that peace was what the people wanted. Both Indian and Pakistani politicians were roundly cursed with the same gaalis. Milan Kundera has written that 'Obscenity is the root that attaches us most deeply to our homeland.' If our gaalis are the same, how distant can our roots be?

At times, the people-watching was more interesting than the match. You couldn't take your eyes off the upper class women, with their heavy make-up, jewellery and even heavier

Dravid charmed by a shopkeeper

adda. The middle class and lower middle class girls were the true surprise. Despite a noticeable financial gap, you could see that they had spent time in putting themselves together. Since showing any skin is taboo, the sexiness is played out in the subtlest way. Narrow shalwars, cut in the spiciest manner, ride up to show not only an enticing ankle but halfway up the calf when they sit. Slits of long kurtas run high to expose the outside of the thigh all the way to the waist. And, with the clingy fabric they choose, it is obvious that under all that cover up, they are wearing thongs. No granny panties here! One young woman had tiny, laced pompoms on the sides of her slim pajamas that popped out when she sat down and lay hidden when she stood up. The intricacies of enticement were laid out like a strategic battle plan.

None of this could have been experienced sitting in an exalted box, where interaction with regular Pakistanis was impossible. In the evening, we were in for a treat. Visiting sports manager Lokesh Sharma in his hotel room, we met the two stars of that day's match. Rahul Dravid, supremely calm and relaxed, sitting quietly, yet open to discussing the match in detail. Mohammed Kaif walked in with bare feet, wearing baggy shorts and a loose T-shirt. He sat down on the floor for a shared dinner. Dravid and Kaif both smirked listening to Sunil Gavaskar pontificating on the match on television. I asked Dravid, 'When the ball is coming at you, it seems like a bullet to a soldier. Do you have time to react with the detailed technique Gavasker is talking about or is it just wild instinct?' 'When you train enough then your instinct will use the right technique for that particular ball,' he replied.

Instead of hitting the party circuit that night, we opted to go to Kuku's Café. According to urban legend, the son of a prostitute owns the restaurant and, we are told, his sister is also a prostitute. It is located on Food Street. As we walk around we are indeed surprised that this was obviously a home owned by a wealthy Hindu. Statues of Hanuman and other gods and goddesses are still embedded in the walls. What is even more surprising is that there are diyas lit in homage in front of each statue. You climb up four steep and narrow stone steps to the roof terrace. The backdrop is a massive masjid, exotically lit, with one minaret very close to us. The restaurant has no kitchen. Reading the menu (in Urdu and requiring translation from the waiter) is the one time we feel like foreigners. You choose the dish you want and it is brought from the dhabas lining Food Street. Then, it is pulled up in a basket from the ground floor, with the waiter hanging precariously over the balcony. The food is sublime; the clean night sky full of blinking stars and the cool breeze from the masjid makes you believe in God again.

There is a group of young people on the table next to us.The clothes they wear, the way they talk, hooking up on cell phones for the next hangout, they could be from any city in India.

Despite all the honour killings, lack of equal rights in courts and the ability of men to implement instant divorce with just three words, one noticed that the men were gently protective of their women, taking care of them as though they were wrapped in cotton wool. One was struck by the contrast, watching brothers taking care of their sisters. There were separate counters for women everywhere, from the airport to ticket counters.

Weren't these the same people who came out in hordes in marches against India and burned our flag? Hadn't Indians done the same thing? How could everybody change so fast? Politicians decided to open the door a chink and the people of both countries have pushed the door wide open and barged through.

Before we leave, two Pakistani women arrive in boutique owner Kavita Bhartia's hotel room with three suitcases crammed with embroidered kurtas and shalwars. Despite the city of Lahore looking charmingly as it did ten years ago, the spirit of enterprise is catching on. There are no Ansal Plaza malls assaulting your senses. Shopping is still done in old-style markets with stand-alone one-storey stores. There are no traffic jams and the roads are clean, lined with trees everywhere. In the one hour we have to shop before boarding the flight back, shopkeepers treat us with utmost charm. Knocking down prices, they tell us, 'You are our guests'; phoning up friends to come and meet the visiting Indians. Why wouldn't they want peace between the two countries if both could enjoy the fruits of commerce and trade? What is worrying is, when the Pakistanis visit us, will we be able to reciprocate with the same graciousness?

The nervous question then rankles: Is this change of heart long-term? Could this hope to be like Russia's *perestroika* and *glasnost*, once let out of the bottle, impossible to go back again in time? If the politicians change their minds and become hostile again, will the people regress to mistrust and suspicion? People to people contact is all about emotion and personal relationships. Can we turn it on and off like a tap? But if the people's feelings and demand for peace are strong enough, can it prove as powerful a platform for popularity for the leaders of both countries as jingoistic wars prove to be?

The door that has been opened has a strong wind blowing through it and it is going to be difficult to close it again. That is, one hopes it will be difficult. Should one be cautious and not get carried away with cricket euphoria? Hope in some way is always naive, but that should not negate it. Watching this cricket match, you were not just watching a cricket match. You were participating in a change of policy between two nations. You were not in the mahawl (ambience); you made and became the mahawl.

More than Cricket:

In Karachi & Beyond

Nina Martyris

On my very first morning in Karachi, that sprawling seaside city which once was capital of the new state of Pakistan before upstart Islamabad sprang out of Rawalpindi's side, I was shanghaied by the famous *mehman nawazi* that is now a fabled part of subcontinental lore. Indians aren't exactly slobs in the hospitality trade, and centuries of dutiful obeisance to the guest, be it Huien Tsang or the Dalai Lama, has earned us a more flattering slot on the hospitality index than on the transparency one. But, from the pen of one still struggling to extricate herself from the bear hug of neighbourliness, be warned that Pakistani chivalry threatens to outclass. If you happen to be Indian in Pakistan, there is no asylum that will shelter you from this wide-eyed hospitable gaze, as I was to discover to both my joy and consternation over my ten-day tour of Karachi, Rawalpindi and Peshawar.

So there I was, two days before the Ides of March, chatting up fans outside the National Stadium before the first cricket match between the two nuclear neighbours was scheduled to spark. A massive river of fans was pouring in, thick rivulets of men in scraggly beards and airy Pathan suits, a bus of rowdily silent hearing-impaired children, a set of dentists in jeans with their cheeks pancaked with crescents, girls in green chic, always in groups, never alone, big fat mamas in mehendi, and chipper expat students who yelled with the arrogance of the well-heeled, 'We love Pakistan, we love India, we hate Thackeray, we hate Modi.'

Celebrity box: Sunil Shetty, Gautam Singhania, Mandira Bedi, Imran Khan and Shoaib Akhtar

I noticed that two boys, whom I later got to know really well as Fawad Hussain and his slightly older friend Faisih Amjed, were studying the press identity card that I had slung around my neck like a badge of courage with much curiosity. Their Hilfiger caps and Fila trousers betrayed their salubrious Clifton or Defence address (posh neighbourhoods in Karachi), as did their accented English, an indecipherable register of Clifton and Texan. I waited for the question and it came, sprayed with the requisite dash of wonderment. From India? Bombay, I said, and sat back smugly in my mind waiting for the Pavlovian effect that I knew this association with Shangri-La would awaken in the veins of young male Pakistanis who have never visited this burdened, heroic city except via their dreams and the 70 mm screen.

If I had said Mars or New York or London I would have lost my audience right away. But I had said Bombay. Bling bling. Within minutes of being asked whether or not I had met various filmstars and being told that he was the proud owner of a bottle of Shah Rukh perfume, Fawad stuttered out a proposition. It wasn't a marriage proposal, but it was as suicidal. Would I join him, his cousins and friends in the stands to see for myself, first-hand, how much Pakistanis love Indians? Sorry, I said, I don't have a ticket, and pointed by way of explanation to my plastic ID pendant which parochially stated Press Box. No problem, said Fawad, whipping out a Rs 1,500 ticket from his Fila pocket. It was a ticket to the VIP Imran Khan enclosure, something any cricket fan would kill for, and I was acutely aware of the honour that had been extended.

Apart from being thrown by this show of generosity from one so young, my radar of self-protection, good Indian that I was, was beeping madly. Would I be the sole Indian amidst a sea of green? What if things turned ugly and India won? What if there were only men in the

Shukla, Dalmia, Jaitley, Priyanka with brother Rahul Gandhi and husband Robert Vadra

stands? The City of Jinnah or *Shere e-Qaid*, as Karachi is sonorously known by its Urdu title, was no Disneyland. It was a city with a rather scary reputation for violence, and only last night I had sat rivetted through Kamila Shamsie's *Kartography,* a novel on how years of sectarian attrition had redrawn the map of her beloved city. Ever since a bomb in the summer of 2002 had claimed the lives of eleven French engineers outside the Karachi Sheraton, forcing the New Zealand team to call off its tour, the city had become something of an untouchable on the international cricket circuit.

But when a ninth standard boy who wears his cap back to front is doing his bit for Indo-Pak relations, only a churl or coward would refuse. Thank you, I said, and battened down the voices of warning that family and friends had seen me off with, chief among them being, don't go alone to the stands. My apprehensions were, of course, gloriously unfounded. The boys and I were initially a little concerned about my ID card shouting out my nationality but I soon found that it worked to my advantage. Guards, commandos and rangers parted like the Red Sea to allow me right of passage, closing in officiously on Fawad and Faisih who were trotting in my wake. The stands, overwhelmingly Pakistani (what else did I expect?), were tousled with emotion. A boisterous positivism glittered in the air, as did a nervous patter that was to later vroom into hysteria. Patriotism was doing its push-ups preparing for the big match ahead. But above all, as was evident from the reassuring scattering of peace posters, there was a boyscout eagerness to prove to the Doubting Thomases of the world that the Karachi cricket stand was not some outpost of hooliganism, but a mature sporting forum where cricket lovers came together to support the game and help build peace muscle as well. It was almost as if every

Rooting for cricket: Indo-Pak solidarity

single person present saw it as his or her personal duty to launder the city's stained cricket bona fides.

The stadium wasn't a male preserve either, as the Arbab Niaz Stadium in the mountain-rimmed township of Peshawar turned out to be with its separate enclosure for the *khawateen* (women). Here, the VIP stands were sequined with the beauties of Karachi, their large sunshades nestling midst mehendied locks, their stilettos supporting groomed feet that had not seen too much sun. A local celebrity fashion choreographer even turned up in a patchwork velvet top hat. 'Joker. Thinks she's at the derby or what?' said one of Faisih's friends. Shortly afterwards, the top hat disappeared.

The Karachi one-dayer will go down in cricketing history as much for its hair-raising 5-run finale in India's favour as for the impeccable behaviour of 33,000 fans who cheered their home team with whoops of hysteria but stood up in one accord to applaud Rahul Dravid to the pavilion when he was cruelly nicked by Shoaib Akhtar at 99. Not once did I hear a single anti-India slogan or taunt. All through the match strangers walked up to me to exchange e-mail addresses, and the next day two of them, a Rotarian and a hydrologist, did e-mail, inviting me home. Personally for me the most touching moment came when a lady in a silk salmon shalwar sitting in the row behind me, discerned my isolation and tapped me on the shoulder and said, 'Don't be afraid. *Aap India ke liye nare lagaye. Hum saath denge.*' After that I did not feel so afraid.

I was probably the only Indian in the enclosure that day but there were at least three tricolours being waved, all by young Pakistani nationals. Would Wankhede Stadium or Eden Gardens wave the Pakistani flag? I doubted it very much. One particularly billowy tiranga jhanda was held aloft by a quartet of stockbrokers from the Karachi stock exchange. Another discoloured khadi flag was worn by a schoolboy on his back, 'for friendship', he told me perspiring in the heat as he ran up and down the stands. He explained that he had given his Pakistan flag to an Indian fan in exchange for the khadi one. This is more than one had hoped for – even cricket had its uses, I decided magnanimously.

And then, in the midst of the cricket and peace lust, for a span of ten minutes, the great game was pushed down the pecking order. 'Gandhi's daughter,' yelled Faisih Bhai, excitedly, pointing to the adjacent enclosure where Priyanka and Rahul Gandhi stood, waving in the sunlight to the heads below in the tradition of their parents, grandmother and great-grandfather (Gandhi children by now are genetically programmed to wave and an imperious wave is probably the first thing a Gandhi baby does to announce its arrival). I did not ask what they meant by 'Gandhi's daughter', and who the Gandhi was that they were referring to. 'Oh man, I heard she's gorgeous,' said Ahmed Bhai, straining to get an eyeful. The presence of Jawaharlal Nehru's two great-grandchildren on this historic match day was like a benediction, as was that of Mohammed Ali Jinnah's scions Dina Wadia and Nusli Wadia two weeks later at the Lahore one-dayer. Priyanka, whom veteran Pakistani cricket commentator Omar Kureishi described as 'an elfin-like Audrey Hepburn' seemed intent on giving her security team of seven guards a nervous breakdown by insisting on spending 20 minutes with the plebs in the stands – her Karachi Holiday turn, if you like. What followed was the theatre of the absurd. When Priyanka leapt up on her chair to cheer, the seven stalwarts hopped agitatedly on to chairs behind, when Snow White sat down, they sat down too.

Even Indian political royalty couldn't distract from the pitch fever. As the match reached its climatic run, it seemed like Pakistan would do the impossible and breach India's magnificent 349 total. Before my eyes the mood changed from hope to hysteria. I started feeling very

Indian. 'Pakistan Zindabad' hammered the air as did cries of 'Allah-o-Akbar'. The men were dancing on their seats, hammering victory rhythms on the plastic chairs, rasping through paper trumpets, hugging one another, thumping their Wolverine boots on the steps. Faisih, who had been providing me with a parallel commentary all through the match on the virtues of peace between the two countries, mercifully forgot all about saving the world and screamed himself hoarse. The Karachi stockbrokers who had held up the Indian flag despite the stream of paper planes and Pepsi cups that had been hurled at them through the day by less liberal fists, continued to wave it bravely, although their faces glowed with the hope that Pakistan might save the day. As Ashish Nehra's ball spun through the evening air, we could see an agitated coach Javed Miandad gesticulating wildly from the pavilion willing Moin Khan to do a repeat of Miandad's 1986 Sharjah knock and send the ball spinning for a six.

But it was the day of the *mehman*. Nehra's ball took Moin's wicket and closed the match. Fawad, Faisih and their friends were frozen, like their hero Shah Rukh in so many tragedy films, except that here they weren't hamming. The euphoria was sucked away, the stadium collapsed on itself. Cricket may have won and peace may have triumphed, but the sons of the soil had lost the first match. It was a hard blow, and I slunk away, unwilling to put my hosts through the ordeal of congratulating me, which as good hosts, they would have done. There was no tear gas to control the crowds this time, only tears, and I did not want to be the cross-border witness.

In Rawalpindi and Peshawar I watched the match from the stands too, but the electricity of Karachi was missing. Or perhaps it had to do with the fact that India lost in both these cities. Or perhaps it was because I was alone and not a part of a group who had shared biryani and Pepsi with me. Outside the Rawalpindi stadium, young boys in Pathan suits and sneakers hung around, hoping to sneak past the guns and uniforms and get a glimpse of their Rawalpindi Express in action, but there was no sneaking past security on this tour. Even President Musharraf had to buy a ticket, or so we were told. In the frontier town of Peshawar, I watched from the Khatun Enclosure, my dupatta draped around my head although there were many bare-headed women present. More than half the stands were taken up by women commandos in black uniforms with matching lipstick and nail polish – the women police officers told me that they even had a make-up allowance which was later discontinued much to their chagrin. The Peshawari women were quieter, their body language less assertive than that of their Karachi cousins. The cheering was muted but one of them had brought a home-made English poster along, which popped up from time to time: Do you still think we are unsafe? it asked, mirroring the hurt of a proud host that had been considered suspect. I also remember how disappointed Shaukat Bhai, the manager of Pearl Guest House where I was staying was, when Sachin got out on a duck. He had bought a ticket only to watch Tendulkar bat, he said crestfallen, and he had to go and get out on zero.

I, too, remain indebted to a schoolboy for inviting me to watch the match from the stands instead of the Press Box with its laptop languor and gratuitous opinions. Just chatting with the teenagers about their lives helped to detonate the various myths that one labels Pakistan with and also get a pulse of their feelings for Big Brother India. It was here that I learnt that the tent-like canopies worn by Afghani women were called shuttlecock burqas because of their shape, that Atal Bihari Vajpayee was respected and Bal Thackeray disliked because he dug up pitches, that anger at the way Muslims had suffered in Gujarat was still alive, that ABN-Amro was the biggest foreign bank here, that the rich went hunting with packs of Pointers and German Shepherds and threw away the wild boar they killed since no one eats pork in Pakistan 'except the American embassy', that Nana Patekar was a hero in Kabul, that the Karachi brat pack had dance-and-barbecue parties at a place called French Beach to the beat of *Kaanta Laga*, that the Sunjay Dutt film *Munna Bhai MBBS* had completely captured the public imagination so that when Shahid Afridi missed a catch the crowd yelled, 'Arre Mamu, vaat lag gayi.' And it was here that I heard the fascinating term 'naked eyes', a term that stayed in my mind, because it told of a society still folded in conservatism despite the beach parties and raunchy videos. 'Of course women in burqas drive,' Fawad informed me. 'They may be covered, but their eyes are naked.'

Naked eyes: Cricket through the veil

'India+Pakistan= World Power'

Kadambari Murali

The high point of this series for me happened right at the beginning, in Karachi, during that first intoxicating one-dayer. If you weren't one of the blessed, sitting there among the 35,000-odd people who had squeezed into the National Stadium, you had missed out on one of life's big experiences. But I'm getting ahead in my story. The context of the almost tangibly tense atmosphere that hung over Pakistan's business capital during those two days of March that the Indian team and its extended caravan descended on it, goes back some way. To February, when the security expert among the team of three officials on a reconnaissance mission for the BCCI (Board of Cricket Control in India) and Indian government 'recommended' that Karachi should not host a Test match (the Pakistan Cricket Board had wanted the first Test to be in Karachi).

The recommendation was more or less a diktat of sorts. Even as we reporters were doing story after story trying to gauge which way the series would go, we all knew that whatever happened, Karachi and Peshawar were out for the Tests.

When the team got back, and the usual confabulations were done with, a joint secretary in the sports ministry sent a letter to Jagmohan Dalmiya with the government's recommendation that the tour go ahead but with certain clauses. One of them was the Karachi one.

It was a decision that, at the time, we were expecting and didn't react much to – there was no point wasting time over a futile argument. The PCB was expecting it too but they were not happy. I remember talking to a senior PCB official at the time and he was very upset. 'Why are there two standards for India and Pakistan?' he asked. 'The last major bomb blast in the region was outside the Taj hotel in Mumbai, not the Sheraton in Karachi. New Zealand still

SUPERSTITIONS

■ Rahul Dravid is very careful about putting his right foot first on the ground when he comes in to bat. He also takes a fresh guard for each new bowler.

■ Mohinder Amarnath always has a red handkerchief tucked nonchalantly in his pocket when he goes to bowl. Recently, Sourav Ganguly and Virender Sehwag have been carrying this tradition forward.

■ Sourav Ganguly carries a photograph of his guruji when he is playing. Further more, he has also changed the number of his shirt after his early failures. He still wears the number 99 when in the field, but when it comes to batting, Ganguly dons a shirt with the number 24 on its back.

■ Sunil Gavaskar always used to ground his bat first before bringing his

came to India. You will still have matches in Mumbai.' PCB chief Ramiz Raja also said more in the same vein.

And the people of Karachi were extremely hurt. How much they were hurting we realized only when we went there for the first one-day game. And how embarrassed we were made to feel by the grace with which they reacted to what, in their eyes, would definitely have been a slight.

The city was festooned with blue and white banners that had signs like 'Games and sports for love and peace,' 'Karachi welcomes our Indian guests' and 'We welcome the Indian cricket team.' Lahore, where we landed, had no obvious signs (other than at the official hotel) that a significant series was in the offing. Karachi was an utter surprise and a great start. Everyone from the uniformed cleaners sweeping spotless roads to the big-built armed Pakistan Rangers and machine gun-wielding cops on moving cars constantly scanning everything, wanted to chat and offer help the minute they realized you were from India.

But the most emotive manifestation of the whole thing was left to that perfect, perfect one-day game at the National Stadium, one that many said could have been scripted by the gods.

It was a wicket that had been made for batsmen to entertain the crowd, and that they did. Batting first and with Sachin Tendulkar and Virender Sehwag going berserk (nearly 70 runs in 9 overs), India started with flamboyant flair. Tendulkar fell at that point but Sehwag continued to bash the much-vaunted Pakistan attack to finish with 79 off 57 balls.

There was Sourav Ganguly's smooth 45 off 47 balls and a

A sentiment which speaks for itself

vital, century partnership between two of the coolest characters in the team – Rahul Dravid (99 off 104 balls) and Mohammed Kaif (46 off 56).

Inzy's son meets Sachin

India landed up making 349 and when Zaheer Khan and L. Balaji gave away only 40 runs or so in the first 10 overs and accounted for both openers, their fans could have been forgiven for thinking that this one was in the bag.

But everyone had reckoned without Inzamam ul-Haq, that gentle mountain of a man who was once unanimously acclaimed as a genius at par with Tendulkar and Brian Lara. Inzamam, the butt of some malicious criticism in the media from various quarters as this series progressed, played that day in Karachi with exquisite flair and an almost contemptuous disdain for the intimidating target and the Indian bowlers.

His 104-ball 122 and two crucial century partnerships with Yousuf Youhana (73) and Younis Khan (46) made this Pakistan chase the highest ever one-day total by a team batting second and took them to within 5 runs of India's huge total.

It would have been an unprecedented, almost unbelievable victory. That it was not was finally due to two things. An almost mind-boggling catch by Kaif, who sped in from long off towards mid-on, dived headfirst to avoid colliding with Badani – it was an incredible sight, one body smoothly sailing over the other – and managed to hold on to one of the best catches we will probably ever see.

The other critical performance was from another youngster thought to have a brilliant future when he first

right foot into position, taking guard.

- Sachin Tendulkar always straps on his left pad first. During his captaincy, Sachin would never take off his playing gear, even after his dismissal.

- Imran Khan wore a tiger T-shirt in the finals of the 1992 World Cup to bring him luck.

- Mohammed Azharuddin always wore his *taveez* hanging out of his shirt when he went to bat.

- K. Srikkanth always looked at the sun as he went in to the field, wore his left pad first and always walked to the right of his partner while opening the innings.

- Yuvraj Singh believes that the bandana he wears brings him good luck.

- Ashish Nehra does not enter the field

SUPERSTITIONS

without first touching the ropes lining the boundary.

- Harbhajan Singh does not start his day without reciting '*nitnaam*' (daily prayer) and it has been a practice with him ever since his father passed away in 2001.

- Australian sports psychologist Sandy Gordon provided the Indian team theme 'Now or Never'. The cricketers penned down their personal goals after one-to-one sessions with Gordon. The Indian team is not going into any match in this event without putting their signatures onto a white sheet of paper inscribing the team theme. Although this was a motivational method, members of the Indian team now religiously follow the practice of putting their signatures on the white sheet before going to play.

came, but plagued intermittently by injuries that have made him fluctuate between performances of near genius and obviously unfit, indifferent stuff.

Pakistan needed nine runs to win off the last over when Ashish Nehra came on to bowl. With Pakistan coach Javed Miandad excitedly waving his arms from the dressing room balcony, everyone watching was bound to remember Miandad's own last-ball exploits at Sharjah that probably made Chetan Sharma a mental wreck for a while and impacted India's cricketing psyche for years.

But Nehra – and god only knows what he was going through – bowled an over that was never really duplicated in this series, despite some magnificent moments, for the sheer pressure and atmosphere it was bowled under. Pakistan lost the game by three runs.

Even as the match ended, the Karachi crowd spontaneously stood up and applauded the Indian players in a gesture that perhaps, will forever symbolize a new beginning. The Indians too applauded that gracious crowd as they walked off the field. Many would later say that they had never had quite the same feeling anywhere.

A couple of days after we left the port city, emotionally drained but on an inexplicable high, came the news that a huge cache of RDX had been found outside the US consulate

Rawalpindi Express bowls Sehwag out

Tense times: Miandad directs his team. 1st ODI Karachi

there, something to do with General Musharraf's visit or perhaps, US Secretary of State Colin Powell's. Many of us nervously joked that whoever had planned it was kind enough to wait for all the Indians in town to leave the city. A Pakistani journalist who heard us laughed and said, 'They probably did. Only you guys think that Pakistani people have a problem with you. Many are anti-American, but other than some fanatics, no one is anti-India.'

We were to find that sentiment repeated as we moved through Pakistan. As for Karachi, all of us wished that we had the advantage of hindsight and had been able to witness a Test

Nehra bowls winning over: 1st ODI Karachi

SUPERSTITIONS

■ Anil Kumble fondly remembers how Sachin Tendulkar used to come running, take Kumble's sweater and hand it to the umpire during the Delhi Test against Pakistan. Sachin's superstition proved correct; Kumble registered a perfect 10, claiming all Pakistani wickets and guiding India to a historic win!

■ Most of the cricketers have their own spots in the various dressing rooms, around the country and around the world. For example, on Sunday's ODI match, V.V.S. Laxman was asked not to leave his seat till the match got over. There is a feeling in the team that India wins whenever Laxman sits in a particular place and watches the whole match. In fact, he spent the whole NatWest Trophy sitting in one position! After his dismissal, Yuvraj Singh got onto the massage table; soon after that,

SUPERSTITIONS

the scoring rate picked up through Mohammed Kaif and Rahul Dravid. As he was about to get up, he was told to keep lying down. Only when the chase got easier and the target closer was he allowed to get up!

■ During Sunday's match, Ganguly and Tendulkar asked media manager Amrit Mathur to stay away from the changing room. The reason: a wicket would fall every time Mathur was in the room!

■ Some cricketers refuse to shave in the midst of a good run, and others wear the same pants for several matches all together, the fear being that by washing them, they may wash their luck away as well!

■ With nothing going right for the Pakistani cricketers against India, a local Pakistani newspaper suggested some senior cricketers

there. It is a living, breathing city that also loves its cricket. It was bustling with life and a joie de vivre that we never found anywhere else in Pakistan. Even though Lahore, which most of our motley crew came to think of as a home of sorts, had a comfortable, uncomplicated atmosphere, there was no question that the Karachi experience was the most potent expression of what this tour was supposed to be about – the coming together of two warring nations, at least of two peoples.

For me, one of the quirkier moments of the tour happened in Islamabad, just before the second one-day international at Pindi (Rawalpindi). I was getting into the lift at the Marriot hotel and was followed in by Rahul Dravid and Amrit Mathur, the BCCI's director communications, who was the team's media manager for the tour. Just as the doors were about to close, I saw a Pakistani player running towards the lift, so I pressed the button to hold on. It was Pakistani batsman Yasir Hameed, who had not done anything of note in Karachi.

He walked in and politely smiled all around. Dravid, the quintessential gentleman, probably felt that he had to respond. To my utter bewilderment, he told Hameed, 'You bowled very well at the nets today.' Hameed looked a little confused and before he could say anything, the Indian vice-captain put his foot in further by asking if he was 'Saqlain's brother'. I just about heard Yasir reply 'Actually, I'm an opening batsman,' when my floor came and I couldn't hear the end of this fascinating conversation.

Two days later, even as Shahid Afridi (eventually out for 80) tore the Indian bowling to shreds, Yasir, at the other end, played a superb mature innings to top score in the game with 86. Their opening partnership of 80 off the first 10 overs gave rise to speculation that this match might well see a repeat of Karachi, this time for Pakistan.

But another superb spell from Nehra brought on after Balaji and Zaheer were mauled, (3 for 44 in his 10 overs), made sure Pakistan only got to 329. India were always looking at a difficult task.

But Pakistan had not reckoned with a man called Tendulkar. This innings, as those in the recent past after he

Jubilant Afridi gets Ganguly: 2nd ODI, Pindi

firmly established himself alone atop cricket's pantheon, was not the demolition attack that used to send the opposition into collective, hysterical depression.

It was a slow, careful start in which he restricted shots that have led him into trouble, interspersed with blazing boundaries that made those fielding remember who he was.

But whether he obliterates them or not, Tendulkar dampens the spirits of the opposition just by being at the crease. So the Pakistani players could be forgiven the almost manic joy with which they celebrated the moment when Tendulkar walked off the field after Abdul Razzaq at mid-wicket, held on to a catch off Shoaib Malik.

Dravid, who had been involved in a century stand with Tendulkar, fell soon after, as did Yuvraj and Kaif. Ramesh Powar, in his debut match, and Balaji, whose name was being

sporting beards should shed their 'facial growth' and follow the clean-shaven approach of Indian cricketers to make a fresh bid to regain lost prestige. Having a dig at the cricketers with beards, the newspaper said 'after the Taliban made the absence of a beard punishable with whiplashes, the religious beard has crept into Pakistani cricket. Pakistan's Saeed Anwar allowed himself a flowing one, but alas, did not do well on the field after that.'

In Pakistan, on the eve of the second ODI in Rawalpindi, a band of bird-lovers set free 10,000 mynahs in Karachi and Lahore for Pakistan to win the second one-dayer. 'With such a big series being played, we decided to do that for Pakistan to win in the second match,' said one of one of them. 'It is not a sure shot method but we have seen miracles happen.'

SUPERSTITIONS

Heroes of the One-day Internationals 2004

Sachin Tendulkar

213 RUNS IN FIVE MATCHES IS LITTLE TESTIMONY TO Sachin Tendulkar's credentials. As a senior member of the side, Tendulkar knew a lot rested on him for India to do well in the five-match Samsung Cup series. After promising much in the opening ODI in Karachi, Tendulkar came into his own with a masterly crafted 141 in the second tie in Rawalpindi. It was for a lost cause, though, as India lost the tie. But was anybody complaining? It came off just 135 balls and contained 17 fours and a six. Everyone expects Tendulkar to play like Virender Sehwag. With age, his reflexes are slower and nowadays he is there to anchor the innings. In the fifth ODI, Tendulkar took an astonishing catch on the long-on fence to send back Pakistan captain Inzamam-ul-Haq. That was the turning point of the series which India won 3-2.

Irfan Pathan

HE'S THE NEW PIN-UP BOY OF INDIAN CRICKET. ALL OF 19 and willing to learn, Pathan could end up as the find of the tour. Like Kapil Dev when India toured Pakistan in 1978. After a highly successful tour of Australia, Pathan was dropped for the first two matches. It was indeed a shocking decision and many former cricketers including Ravi Shastri and Ian Chappell were questioning the basis on which he was made to sit out. Pathan came into the side for the third match after Ashish Nehra pulled with an injury. He finished with 8 wickets which in itself was a statement. Pathan was the leading wicket-taker amongst the Indian bowlers. The second-best was Zaheer Khan who had 7 wickets but played in all five matches. In the fifth ODI, Pathan bowled brilliantly for a tally of 10-1-32-3 and there were many who believed that he, and not V.V.S. Laxman who belted a century, should have been the man of the match.

Mohammad Kaif

YOU CAN EXPECT TWO THINGS FROM THIS ALLAHABADI – a quick 50 and quicksilver movements on the field that will save at least 30-odd runs. There are ODI specialists in every team and Kaif is our trumpcard. Kaif is a slow starter but once he does that there is only the fourth gear. Kaif played a superlative innings in the fourth match at Lahore. When everything seemed lost, he joined hands with Dravid to take India to victory. His 71 off 79 balls with eight boundaries saw India win the match handsomely and also tie the series 2-2 to make the fifth ODI interesting. Memories of this historic series will fade away, but one will remain forever etched in everyone's mind. That's the brilliant catch Kaif took to send back Shoaib Malik in the first ODI at Karachi. Even a minor collision with Hemang Badani did not prevent him from dropping the ball. He held on to it for dear life.

V.V.S. Laxman

A KNEE PROBLEM KEPT HIM OUT OF THE FIRST ODI IN Karachi. The injury to Hemang Badani brought Laxman into the side for the second ODI. Despite scoring three centuries in the Tri-series in Australia recently, Laxman was not always assured of a place in the first eleven. Everybody felt that for a man in poor touch, the dressing room was the best place. But Laxman answered his critics in brilliant fashion. He came good when it mattered most, in the final, with a breathtaking century. Laxman's classy 107 off 104 balls with 11 silken boundaries had everyone raving about the knock. The 'oohs' and 'aahs' were back. Laxman batted the way only he can. What was important that the knock helped India pile up a near-300 total and proved to be a match-winning one. Laxman was, of course, declared Man of the Match.

NOVEMBER 3, 1978 AT ZAFAR ALI STADIUM, SAHIWAL

When 23 runs were required from 14 balls with 8 wickets in hand (183/2 off 37.4 overs) in response to Pakistan 205/7 (40 overs), Indian skipper Bishen Singh Bedi called his batsmen from the field in protest against the persistent short-pitched bowling of speedster Sarfraz Nawaz. The bowler's last four deliveries were all bouncers that had not been called wide by umpires Javed Akhtar and Khizer Hayat.

FEBRUARY 20, 1999 AT EDEN GARDENS, CALCUTTA

Riots were caused first by Sachin Tendulkar's run-out in the second innings on 9, after he had collided with a fielder while completing the third run, and later by India's impending defeat. A few officials witnessed the final 10 balls after a three-hour

Nehra bowled Sami: 2nd ODI, Rawalpindi

chanted by a section of the enthusiastic crowd at that rather unimpressive stadium – it's like Ferozeshah Kotla before the ongoing revamp – attempted to fight back but it was too much for them. India fell short by 12 runs, bowled out for 317.

Against the backdrop of the match – and wondering what was going through Dravid's head even as he kept wickets all the while that Yasir was at the crease – the Dravid-Yasir lift incident was too good a story to miss but I still wondered whether I should mention it in my report for the *Hindustan Times.* Finally, I didn't, not that time.

But Yasir hadn't finished with his revenge. It seemed like an elaborate plan of sorts. In the next game at Peshawar, his hometown, he top-scored again, leading Pakistan to another victory and getting them 2-1 ahead in this absorbing series.

It was quite an amazing performance from Yasir, who almost single-handedly led Pakistan to this win.

But it came later. India might well have lost the game when they lost their top three batsmen with less than 40 runs on board. There were also just 12 scoring shots off the bat from the first 10 overs. In one-day cricket, on any surface, that's not very encouraging! For the first time, there was a wicket on which the seam bowlers benefitted tremendously early, though it became easier to bat on later. Still it wasn't the horror wicket that the Indian top order collapse made it out to be.

This game, incidentally, was preceded by the only slight Pakistan-India controversy on this tour, when Ganguly, responding to a question on Shoaib Akhtar's (controversial) action, said it was there for all to see on TV. The Pakistanis were furious and they played that way. Shoaib bowled a magnificent opening spell, one that had been seen only in erratic bits and pieces earlier on the tour.

Coming back to Yasir's knock, it was just completely impressive because of his relative inexperience (a year into international cricket) and the mature way in which he spaced it out. He didn't lose focus of the target, didn't go bang, bang after the bowlers or anything like that – he just made sure he kept the scoreboard moving by rotating the strike and picked up the boundary with some lovely shots through the off-side every now and then.

By the time Yasir got out, the sixth Pakistani wicket to do so, on a heartbreaking two runs short of a century in front of all those who had watched him grow up right here, Pakistan knew they could do it. India still had a chance to wrap this up if they had got through the lower order but a feisty performance by Abdul Razzaq and Moin Khan in an unbeaten partnership of 74 saw the hosts through by four wickets to go 2-1 up in the series.

This time around, I just had to write about the Dravid-Hameed Incident, but I was careful not to mention the name of the Indian player involved, I thought it wouldn't be fair. But then, the next day, I found that a Pakistani English daily, *The News*, had carried a story on the whole incident, with the player's name. I later found out that Yasir himself had told the reporter in question about the incident, saying that it had inspired him to bat better against India in his hometown.

And his hometown was proud of him. Unlike Afridi, who was from Peshawar but had left to pursue his cricket in

delay. All paying spectators were removed.

MARCH 8, 1987 AT GUJARAT STADIUM, MOTERA, AHMEDABAD

On the fourth afternoon of the Test, play was suspended for 50 minutes after a section of the crowd had pelted Pakistan's fielders with stones. Play resumed after tea with six of the visitors wearing helmets.

OCTOBER 1, 1978 AT AYUB NATIONAL STADIUM, QUETTA

The three-match competition involved innings of 40 six-ball overs between the two countries. The four-run win resulted in India's first ODI win against a Test playing nation.

OCTOBER 13, 1978 JINNAH PARK, SIALKOT

India's total of 79 at that time was the lowest in any ODI in Pakistan.

DECEMBER 17, 1982, MULTAN

Zaheer Abbas (118 off 86 balls) posted the fastest recorded century (72 balls) in LOIs until 1988-89. His second wicket stand of 205 with Mohsin Khan equalled the (then) ODI record for any wicket. For the first time two hundreds were made in the same ODI innings, since Mohsin Khan had also made a hundred.

DECEMBER 31, 1982, MULTAN

Shahid Mahboob became the first Pakistani bowler to take a wicket with his first ball in the ODIs.

OCTOBER 2, 1983, JAIPUR

The Jaipur ODI between the two countries became the first ODI in which no balls and wides were debited to bowlers' analyses.

Karachi, Yasir had stayed on to play in this laidback capital of the North-West Frontier Province. Incidentally, Peshawar was the only place in Pakistan that seemed foreign. The people looked different (the Pathans are huge, handsome men), they spoke a different language (Pushtu not the Urdu or Punjabi we heard almost uniformly elsewhere) and they spoke with a different, thicker accent. Even though the newspapers were full of the Pakistan-US operation to flush out militants and stories of how the tribal agencies (the tribal areas of the NWFP are divided into regions called agencies) were in a tumult, we really saw no evidence of any disturbance in Peshawar itself.

Everyone there was obsessed with the cricket match yet, given the tension over staging a match in Peshawar before this series began, there was none of the fanatical obsession with security we had witnessed in Karachi, or even Lahore and Pindi. Kids were roaming all over the vicinity of the Arbab Niaz stadium, the stands themselves were very close to the ground (players' expressions were visible) and it was all very peaceful.

Incidentally, on the flight back from Peshawar, I was sitting in the seat behind Yasir on the tiny Fokker-27 that was hopefully taking us to Lahore (we all thought it looked terribly small). As usual on this flight, as on others through the tour, the captain announced that he was 'deeply honoured' to be transporting the Indian cricketers and then, after someone obviously reminded him, he added that he was happy to be ferrying the Pakistani cricketers too.

By that time, the Pakistani cricketers were obviously used to this kind of almost second-class treatment in their own country. And on that flight at least, they were much too happy to bother with being forgotten by their PIA captain despite winning that game with relative ease.

There was a marked difference between the demeanour of the Pakistani players and the Indian ones. The Pakistani players were joking around, chatting with everyone. The Indian players loosen up when they're alone or with people they know well and are generally very nice young men, but in public they're always (maybe they're taught to be) conscious of their being Indian cricketers. There's a stiffness to them or a complete disinterest in the surroundings or the people around them. There's obviously a line that no one is supposed to cross.

On that flight perhaps, the Indians were down because of the loss but even generally, the Pakistani players (like others across the world apart from India) are more happy-go-lucky and casual, like young men their age are wont to be.

I cannot recall an Indian player flirting with an air hostess in the way Shoaib Malik did when he asked an admiring young air hostess how he was supposed to buckle the seat belt. He

Guests of honour: Indian team on flight to Lahore

was laughing, the rest of the team was laughing. It was harmless fun and the air hostess took it in the same spirit.

As I was saying hello to Yasir (who I had come to know fairly well by then after interviewing him a couple of times), he suddenly said, 'He won't forget me now, will he?' 'Who, Dravid?' I asked. 'Yes,' he laughed, looking completely mischievous.

Interestingly, a week later here in Multan, the venue of the first Test, Dravid walked up to me at an Indian team interaction over dinner with the media. 'You told everyone about the lift incident, didn't you,' he asked laughing. 'No,' I protested. 'Yasir

OCTOBER 31, 1984
JINNAH PARK, SIALKOT

The ODI scheduled and the remainder of the tour were cancelled immediately on receipt of the news of the assassination of Mrs. Indira Gandhi from Delhi.

MARCH 22, 1985, SHARJAH

Imran Khan, in the semi-final match of the Rothmans Four Nations Trophy exploited a damp pitch to claim Pakistan's first 6-wicket analysis – 10-2-14-6. He was deservingly adjudged the Man of the Match. .

APRIL 18, 1986, SHARJAH

In the Australasia Cup at Sharjah on April 18, 1986, Javed Miandad recorded a century off 107 balls before completing an epic victory by hitting the ultimate ball from Chetan Sharma for a six. Pakistan's first success in a major tournament was worth US $ 40,000 in prize money.

MARCH 20, 1987, HYDERABAD

The Hyderabad ODI provided an interesting finish. In reply to India's 212 for six off 44 overs, Pakistan replied with 212 for 7 off 44 overs. However, India won the game by losing fewer wickets. Had Abdul Qadir not attempted a futile second run off the final ball, Pakistan would have won a match tied on runs and wickets by having the higher score after 25 overs.

DECEMBER 18, 1989 MUNICIPAL STADIUM, GUJRANWALA

Sachin Tendukar (16 years 237 days) and Salil Ankola made their ODI debuts in1989. Salil Ankola hit his first ball for six but

did himself, he told Pakistani journalists.' He laughed again and then added, 'I had barely seen him in Karachi…' It was a rhetorical statement but it was clear that Dravid had obviously taken all the ribbing and the reports that followed the incident with great spirit. But then, he's one of a kind.

So from Peshawar, we moved back to home base and the prospect of an India loss even before the series was officially over. It was a depressing thought and some of us would have to keep reminding ourselves that we were neutral and Pakistan had played very well!

The run-up to that unforgettable fourth one-dayer was subdued. There was a tension in the Indian camp even as hundreds of Indian fans poured into Lahore for the one-dayers. Unlike other matches, when the players were roaming around the hotel casually doing this and that, this time around, they kept to their rooms. Coming down to the lobby meant getting mobbed.

But the atmosphere inside the Gaddafi that Sunday was unbelievably electric. In the queues outside, Indians in blue T-shirts joked around with Pakistanis with painted faces, everyone was on a high. A lot of Pakistani youngsters were aggressively stating that their team would end all debate on the day yet some hoped for an Indian win. 'The final one-dayer will be dead otherwise,' said Raza Ali, standing in that queue.

The omens did not bode well for India when Ganguly lost his fourth straight toss in a row and Inzamam opted to make India chase under lights. And the Pakistan captain obviously likes to finish the job because when he came out to bat, he played an innings of such devastation that it left the Indian fielders in some kind of stupor and the top order batsmen (when they came out to bat), looking completely unfocussed.

While the Pakistan skipper's batting has slowly rediscovered its potential of old in patches over the last few series, he has looked in sublime touch against India in this one. His 123 off 121 balls in Pakistan's 293 was almost chanceless and a joy to watch, whoever you were supporting. It seemed that he just had to touch the ball to send it to the ropes or over.

And when India batted, the thought of winning would have been greeted with hysterical laughter at one stage of the match. Pakistan's pace battery came good and the temperamental, dramatic Shoaib, who had surprisingly (and probably following wise counsel) refused to be drawn into the controversy created by Ganguly's references to his action, got going early. Tendulkar lost this battle against him, being forced to edge one to Moin behind the stumps and then, Laxman got a beautiful inswinger that he just couldn't handle.

The Hyderabadi genius, Sehwag, and Ganguly had both

Youhana smashes as Dravid looks on: 1st ODI Karachi

made breezy starts and collapsed quite as quickly under the starless night sky. People were planning to write on the end of a dramatic series when Yuvraj and Dravid came together for their quick 68-run partnership off 66 balls. But on Yuvraj's departure, India still required 132 for a win. Things looked very depressing when Kaif walked in to join Dravid, who was playing a gem of an innings.

It was the stuff dreams are made of. You cannot get two cooler customers than Kaif and Dravid and it was the kind of tense situation tailor-made for their temperaments. It would not have been easy for Kaif being out there – plagued as he

Sachin Tendulkar, was out second ball.

DECEMBER 22, 1989, GADDAFI STADIUM, LAHORE

Imran Khan, Pakistan captain, surprisingly recalled Krish Srikkanth after being adjudged lbw, only to be caught off the very next ball.

JANUARY 21, 2000 HOBART

Abdul Razzaq produced an outstanding all-round performance. First he played a beautiful knock of 70 off 52 balls with the help of two sixes and four fours, enabling his country to post 262 for seven off 50 overs. As India tried to surpass this challenging total, Razzaq produced an exceptional bowling performance with five for 48, restricting the Indians to 230 off 46.5 overs.

MARCH 28, 2004
MULTAN

Many spectators stayed away from the first ever Test between the two countries in Pakistan due to many factors – exorbitant ticket prices, school exams, the climate, as well as the perception that the Test matches were fixed.

Virender Sehwag, the first Indian to post a triple century (309) in Test cricket, surpassed V.V.S. Laxman's record of 281 (vs. Australia at Calcutta in March 2001) as the highest individual innings for India. When Sehwag commenced his journey back after his dismissal, he got a congratulatory message from Laxman, who came next to occupy the crease, while the entire Indian team stood and applauded at the pavilion.

When the Indians amassed 356 for 2 on the first day of the Multan Test, Imran Khan came down

India victorious: Dravid gives thumbs up

was by calls for his head because of some erratic form and coming to Pakistan for his first series in months following a thumb fracture that kept him out of Australia.

Then of course, there's the fact that he is Muslim. It might be politically incorrect to bring this up, and whatever anyone says to the contrary (and whether or not players publicly admit it), whenever Kaif or Irfan or Zaheer perform against Pakistan, they're always doing so under extra pressure. There's always the fear that some rightwing fanatic back in India will make an offcolour remark about why so and so player did badly that will be played back.

But it was an incredible performance from Dravid and Kaif, who ultimately took India to an improbable five-wicket win with an unbeaten sixth-wicket stand and set up a virtual final in the fifth one-dayer.

On Monday, the morning after, the local papers went ballistic, insinuating that the Pakistan Cricket Board had taken the diplomacy issue too far (under direction from the government) and the series had been fixed so it would gain maximum mileage from going into a decider. On Sunday night, in the post-match press conferences, both teams had reacted strongly to the same suggestions from Pakistani scribes.

Inzamam told someone who asked him if Pakistan meant to lose to 'shut up' and Dravid, asked the same question, said: 'God! Someone get this guy out of the room.' By Tuesday, it was clear that the Pakistani camp, hit by the fixing allegations

Kaif raises his bat as India wins 4th ODI, Lahore

and their own dramatic loss after being in a position to wrap up the series, was showing signs of strain.

They were never really in the game in the final despite restricting India to 293, only Laxman really coming good with his run-a-ball 100. Logically, it was a score that they would have fancied getting to, seeing the ease with which India eventually won in the last game. But the chase fell through right at the beginning, even as the moon came up over the night sky in a perfect crescent as darkness fell.

India had their own special weapon: Irfan Pathan. Pathan, who made the Gaddafi Stadium his own with that record 9-16 haul against Bangladesh at the under-19 Asia Cup some months ago, decided it was time for another special.

After Hameed, (Pakistan's Mr Solid in the previous few games), was toppled by Balaji, Pathan struck. The teenager first had Yousuf Youhana plumb in front (9-2), then took out Taufeeq Umar's leg stump (25-3) and finally got Younis Khan to cut one straight to Yuvraj at point. At 58-3, Pakistan were already gone.

Most of the crowd faithfully hung around, watching this game with much the same spirit that crowds here have been watching the series but no one really held out any hope. India ultimately took the Cup and Pakistan's place in the ICC rankings by 40 runs.

The scene in the lobby of the official hotel was like something you see on TV on Oscar night – complete madness, a feisty happiness all around as fans rejoiced in chaotic, emotional frenzy.

heavily on the authorities for overlooking the weakness of the home team.

Skipper Rahul Dravid's aggressive declaration at 675 for 5 prevented Sachin Tendulkar from reaching his fourth double century and his second in successive overseas Tests. However, Sachin was 'taken by surprise' by the timing of the declaration. 'It is disappointing not to have scored the double century,' said Tendulkar.

Heroes of the One-day Internationals 2004

Abdul Razzaq

EARLIER HE WAS A BOWLER WHO COULD BAT A BIT. Now Abdur Razzaq has reversed his role and become a batsman who can bowl a bit. Earlier in New Zealand, a blitzkrieg from Razzaq left the Kiwi bowlers gasping. And India too were at the receiving end during the ODI series here. He scored just 148 runs in the five matches. What was important was that the speed at which it was scored – 27 off 22 balls, 31 off 18, 53 off 52 and 32 off 24. Razzaq scored only five in the final ODI in Lahore. The Peshawar knock (53 off 52) showed the maturing of Razzaq. At 6 for 173, Pakistan were in danger of not reaching India's small target of 244. But in the company of Moin Khan, Razzaq paced the innings to help Pakistan win and take a 2-1 lead in the series.

Yasir Hameed

THE INDIANS WILL NOT FORGET THIS PLAYER IN A HURRY. Hameed made India pay a heavy price for Rahul Dravid not recognizing him. The story goes that Indian media manager Amrit Mathur and Dravid walked past Hameed. The Indian vice-captain asked Hameed if he was a net bowler who had played against them in the first warm-up match. 'It made me resolve to bat well against Indians,' Hameed was to say later. 'I was hungry to score.' He had just seven runs in the first ODI, but a string of 86, 98 and 45 showed the quality of the player. Hameed's driving was impeccable. The Indian fielders could only stand and applaud the promising Pakistani youngster. Hameed failed in the final, scoring only two of five balls. He was bowled by L Balaji. But as the first Test showed, where Hameed got 91 in the first innings, this talented player is bound to make waves. And soon.

Pakistan

Inzamam-ul-Haq

HE MIGHT BE A POOR RUNNER BETWEEN THE WICKETS. He is even worse as a fielder. But give Inzy the bat, and he can bludgeon any attack into submission. The Indians got a firsthand experience in the opening ODI in Karachi. The Indians set up a seemingly impossible target but failed to realize Inzy's resolve. The Pakistani captain batted like one possessed to score 122 brilliant runs off just 102 balls. It was a dream innings not destined to have a fairytale ending as Pakistan lost the match narrowly. Inzy played another memorable knock in the fourth ODI at Lahore under lights. He got another hundred, 123 off 141 balls. Pakistan failed to win as India tied the series 2-2. Both centuries fetched Inzy the Man of the Match and Man of the Series award and prize.

Mohammed Sami

SACHIN TENDULKAR FACED THIS NIPPY FAST BOWLER for his first ball of the ODI series. And what a delivery it was! Pitched short of good length, it seamed away as Tendulkar swished his bat in the air and failed to connect. The collective sigh at Karachi could be heard all the way in Mumbai. Sami has developed into an outstanding fast bowler. During the series against New Zealand he consistently went over 145 kph. He opened the bowling in the first ODI and got two wickets for 74 runs as the Pakistanis were sent on a leather hunt. Sami picked up three for 41 in the second ODI and then finished with 3-63 in the fifth ODI. The runs conceded were high but Sami had the wickets of Tendulkar, Dravid and Kaif. Sami was the highest wicket-taker for Pakistan with a tally of 11.

TURNING POINTS OF ODIs 2004

MARCH 13th

With 8 balls to go, Pakistan are 340 for 6, only 10 balls away from a sensational victory. Shoaib Malik tries to hit Zaheer Khan for a big one. The ball sails over the bowler's head, hangs in the air, and Mohammed Kaif pulls off a spectacular catch.

MARCH 16th

Conceding 15 extras (14 wides and 1 no-ball) by the Indian bowlers,

After the one-day series, when we came into Multan, steeped in history and apparently the base for a number of fundamentalist groups including the Jamaat-e-Islami, we were greeted with the news that no one was to worry, as the Jamaat had assured the cops they would not hassle civilians or guests. Incidentally, this was also the first time I was approached by a man in mufti (outside Multan airport) and asked my name. I was about to ask who he was when my driver whispered 'ISI'. So I began giving my name, but he smiled and marked off something on a sheet and said, 'Yes, I have it, welcome to Multan'.

Pakistan has been an amazing experience – one that no one could have imagined. Chefs in hotels would make special vegetarian food, auto drivers often had to be persuaded to take some money, shops were forever giving discounts, people on the road who you would stop and ask for directions would ask if you were from India. The minute you said yes, it would be the signal to start a detailed conversation.

I can honestly say this: the kind of welcome, the amount of love and affection that we ordinary people – forget the Indian team – got in Pakistan, we are unlikely to get anywhere else in the world. At least I and all the other Indians I interacted with, agreed that we've never felt so much warmth anywhere else that we've travelled, with or without the team.

There have been many discussions I've had with spectators and kids, enthralled with the idea of India, the happening, rocking, big brother across the border. I have been asked questions on everything. There was that exuberant

Fight to the finish: A frame-by-frame account of Balaji's

teenager Tariq Ali in Lahore perkily wanting to know if Shilpa Shetty was 'all natural'.

Along with Tariq was another Lahori, Javed Shah, a Kashmiri, who said he had no quarrel with India. We had a long discussion on the Kashmir issue (it wasn't a banned word as we had been warned when coming into Pakistan) and Shah and many others all wanted to let us know that they wanted peace. They all had a deep interest in Indian politics and wanted to know if the revival of bilateral ties was a BJP ploy pre-elections under American pressure or the real thing. I hadn't a clue, and told them as much.

There was Mohammed Shamim, my cabbie in Karachi, who happily pointed out a tall building with an ostentatious silver crown on top. 'This is Dawood's building,' he said calmly, waiting for my excited reaction. 'There have been two blasts here on the second and eighth floors but no one was killed. There's an ownership struggle here and it is unoccupied.' Dawood supposedly has a house in Karachi's exclusive Clifton area, but many here says he's now somewhere in Africa.

Shamim has taken my number and promised to get in touch once he gets to India. He told me he had once been to India, for a relative's wedding in Saharanpur and planned to go there again if possible.

He also took me to the three temples I visited in the port city, one where I met a third generation Pakistani Gujarati, who asked me how I liked his country. Then there was Raju, the gatekeeper to the Swaminarayan temple with its signs in

apart from the dismissal of Sachin Tendulkar at 245 when well set, the Pakistanis scored a magnificent innings of 141 off 135 balls, clinching the victory of the men in green.

MARCH 19th

Shabbir Ahmed delivers for the Pakistani team: three wickets (India 37/3) and India are fighting a losing battle. They are not yet out – Irfan Pathan sends Afridi and Youhana out. Yasir Hameed saves the day with a solid knock, allowing Razzaq and

crucial run-out in the nail-biting finale of 2nd ODI, Pindi

Historic moment: India celebrates as Balaji takes the last wicket

Moin Khan to keep the chase going. The Indian bowlers don't have enough to fight for.

MARCH 21st

Team India make a happy start with Irfan Pathan's two early strikes. Vice-captain Rahul Dravid leads India to victory with Kaif providing the necessary support: the duo puts 132 incredible runs for the 6th wicket.

MARCH 24th

In over 6.1, Pakistan begin their chase. India's Balaji and Pathan

Urdu opposite the Sindh city courts. He told me he was from Mulund and when I asked him how he was in Marathi, he laughingly replied that he understood but was more comfortable with Urdu.

There was Mohen Lal, who worked in the laundry at the Pearl Continental hotel in Peshawar, who told me how happy he was living in the city that is so linked with Islamic fundamentalists. 'It's a peaceful town, very tolerant,' he said. 'People have just celebrated Holi with me a while ago and I'm always invited to everyone's homes through the month of Ramzaan. There's no need for me to even think of living anywhere else.'

There was Abdul Hamid, the baggage handler in Islamabad airport, whose older brother Jai Pal got left behind in India during the ravages caused by Partition, when his parents moved to what is now Pakistan from Rajori in Jammu. Abdul, born in 1950, promised his mother on her deathbed, that he would go back and find his brother. He did.

And finally, there was Rabia Khan, a middle-aged freelance scribe here in Multan, announcing that all men were 'kameena' and suddenly breaking down and telling me how she wanted to go to India because she had heard women were treated better.

As I write this, the Multan Test is just over. India have managed a first-ever win on Pakistan soil (by an incredible innings and 52 runs), built around the flamboyant, magnificent Sehwag's becoming the first Indian to break the

leading India to a glorious series win, final ODI, Lahore

300-mark. So already, it's been historic in more ways than India playing a Test series in Pakistan after 14 long years. Just over two weeks of this incredible tour are left. And already, I'm feeling somewhat sad.

It'll be good to go home but this journey, more than anything else, has really made me believe that it is not difficult to believe that the people of the two countries share a common ancestry and legacy.

Nothing probably made me feel it more than in the PC hotel in Lahore, after that final one-dayer. Hundreds were milling around the lobby, waiting for the Indian team to return as I walked in. I was immediately greeted like an old friend by the protocol manager, Tariq *saab* – I had been in Pakistan 20 days by then.

We chatted a while and then, wanting to see the reception, I hung around and got into conversation with two young, excited gentlemen. I asked where they were from – one was from Delhi. The other said he was from Moradabad and then, before I could say anything, he launched into a long explanation of where exactly Moradabad was.

In gist, it went like this: 'It's a small town in northern India, near the capital city, Delhi. Very nice place, you must come there sometime,' he said with a smile. 'I really like Lahore,' he suddenly added. 'So where in Pakistan are you from?'

'Delhi actually,' I smiled. 'But it doesn't matter.' And just then, the victorious Indian team walked in, to be greeted with rapturous cries from a lobby full of Indians. And Pakistanis.

strike early to remove Hameed, Youhana and Umar. At 25/3, Pakistan face an uphill climb. Inamam-ul-Haq is out at 87/5 by Kartik, with Sachin taking a breathtaking catch. It's the beginning of the end, and yet another jubilant victory for India.

From Cream Flannels to Blue & Green

Sunil Warrier, Pradeep Vijaykar,
Nitin Naik, Anant Gaundalkar

TENDULKAR
10
SAMSUNG

Born: **August 5, 1972**
Batting style: **Right-handed**
Bowling style: **Right-arm fast**
Playing years: **1988-1999**

One would think that a one-day specialist is a batsman; such were the whimsical selection policies in Pakistan, that they reduced an effective swing bowler to a one-day bowler. Of course, it didn't help that he had to live under the shadows of the two Ws, Wasim Akram and Waqar Younis. Aqib Javed had a fantastic record against India giving a hard time especially to the great Sachin Tendulkar, getting him out leg before wicket or regularly caught behind. He is one amongst many Pakistani cricketers who succeeded in lifting his game when playing against India. Aqib did not play in a single Test against India but in ODIs his bowling average is 7 points better against the arch-rivals at 24.64. His best bowling figures in limited overs cricket came against India at Sharjah in the Wills Trophy final when he claimed 7 for 37 and destroyed India. His spell included a hat-trick of leg before wickets when he got Ravi Shastri, Mohammed Azharuddin and Sachin Tendulkar. He was instrumental in Pakistan winning the World Cup in 1992, handling the absence of Waqar marvellously.

Batting & Fielding	M	Runs	Avg	H.S.	100	50	S.R.	Ct
ODIs	163	267	10.68	45*	--	--	58.68	24
vs India	39	31	5.17	11	--	--	44.93	10
Tests	22	101	5.05	28*	--	--	--	2
vs India	Did not Play							

Bowling	M	Wkts	Avg	Best	5WI	S.R.	E.R.
ODIs	163	182	31.43	7/37	4	44.02	4.28
vs India	39	54	24.65	7/37	3	33.22	4.45
Tests	22	54	34.70	5/84	1	72.56	--
vs India	Did not Play						

Aqib Javed

Abdul Qadir

Born: **September 15, 1955**
Batting style: **Right-handed**
Bowling style: **Right-arm leg break**
Playing years: **1977-1991**

Long after Abdul Qadir will stop playing cricket with his grandchildren, he will still have this story to narrate to them. 'That boy was good. He stepped out to me, the great Abdul Qadir, the greatest leg spinner in the world. Not once but three times. He hit me for three sixes and every time I challenged him, he would jump out and reach beyond hope. I conceded 27 runs in that one over'. He was of course speaking about a 16-year-old Sachin Tendulkar who was on his maiden series in 1989. Qadir would add that he was fortunate that it was only a festival match at Peshawar. The 70s and 80s were completely dominated by fast bowlers but Qadir's emergence as a classical leg spinner gave even the pace-pronged Pakistanis variety. And Qadir had style. His approach to the wicket was almost from a short mid-off and before every delivery he would give the ball a lick. He was very aggressive and batsmen outside the subcontinent were in awe of him. In 1987-88, Qadir mesmerized England in Lahore with a haul of 9 for 56. But he never enjoyed any success against India. Qadir played 16 Tests and had a paltry 27 wickets with not a single five-wicket haul. His best was 4 for 67 in the 1982-83 series.

Batting & Fielding	M	Runs	Avg	H.S.	100	50	S.R.	Ct
ODIs	104	641	15.26	41*	--	--	74.71	21
vs India	19	105	10.50	39	--	--	82.68	4
Tests	67	1029	15.59	61	--	3	--	15
vs India	16	213	19.36	39*	--	--	--	3

Bowling	M	Wkts	Avg	Best	5WI	S.R.	E.R.
ODIs	104	132	26.08	5/44	2	38.64	4.05
vs India	19	16	38.38	3/27	--	48.56	4.74
Tests	67	236	32.81	9/56	15	72.57	--
vs India	16	27	51.52	4/67	--	94.78	--

Born: **June 3, 1966**
Batting style: **Left-handed**
Bowling style: **Left-arm fast**
Playing years: **1984-2002**

Wasim **Akram**

From a lanky tearaway, this left-hander developed into a magnificent top-notch bowler. Injuries plagued Wasim Akram right through his career, but there is yet to be a competitor for his sobriquet, Sultan of Swing. Akram would be remembered for two Indian connections. The first, when he pulled out of the World Cup match against India in Bangalore. There was a controversy over it but the champion left-arm bowler was indeed injured. More recently, when he helped Indian upcoming bowler Irfan Pathan in Australia, national coach Javed Miandad accused him of passing on trade secrets. Akram was only being helpful to a bowler of his ilk. The change in Pathan is quite evident, as very early in his career he has shown the ability to bring the ball into the right-handed batsman. Akram, whose best batting was a monumental 257 not out against Zimbabwe, played 12 Tests against India and claimed 45 wickets. Not a bad average at 28.86. He seemed a natural leader much like Imran Khan but the match-fixing controversies of the 90s gave Akram a bad name. Over the years Akram lost out on speed but pushed himself to complete a 500-wicket landmark in ODIs in the World Cup last year. He is the only player with more than 400 wickets in both forms of cricket.

Batting & Fielding	M	Runs	Avg	H.S.	100	50	S.R.	Ct
ODIs	356	3717	16.52	86	--	6	88.46	88
vs India	48	425	14.17	50	--	1	91.79	14
Tests	104	2898	22.64	257*	3	7	--	43
vs India	12	277	19.79	62	--	1	--	6

Bowling	M	Wkts	Avg	Best	5WI	S.R.	E.R.
ODIs	356	502	23.53	5/15	6	36.23	3.90
vs India	48	60	25.17	4/35	--	40.42	3.74
Tests	104	414	23.62	7/119	25	54.65	--
vs India	12	45	28.87	5/96	2	65.07	--

Mohinder **Amarnath**

Born: **September 24, 1950**
Batting style: **Right-handed**
Bowling style: **Right-arm medium**
Playing years: **1969-1988**

Swing, reverse swing, inverse swing, medium pace, fast bowling, dubious umpiring. Indian batsmen were up against Imran Khan, Sarfraz Nawaz and other Pakistani medium pacers as well as the biased Pakistani umpires on the 1982-83 tour. Our batters were falling like pins on the bowling alley. But one refused to buckle and get knocked down. Mohinder Amarnath played 18 Tests against Pakistan but the 1982-83 series will be best remembered for the exploits of this brave and valiant warrior son of Lala Amarnath. He hooked with aplomb and with such ease that runs simply flowed from his bat. He notched up 584 runs in 6 Tests at an average of 73 with three hundreds and half-centuries apiece. West Indies Master Blaster Vivian Richards rated him as the best player of fast bowling in the 80s. Amarnath, with the red handkerchief jutting out of his pocket, made another century on the truncated 1984-85 series. The Pakistanis could well award him citizenship of their country. He loved their pitches and their bowlers too.

Batting & Fielding	M	Runs	Avg	H.S.	100	50	S.R.	Ct
ODIs	85	1924	30.54	102*	2	13	57.67	23
vs Pakistan	20	471	42.82	88	--	5	62.72	4
Tests	69	4378	42.50	138	11	24	--	47
vs Pakistan	18	1080	45.00	120	4	5	--	12

Bowling	M	Wkts	Avg	Best	5WI	S.R.	E.R.
ODIs	85	46	42.85	3/12	--	59.35	4.33
vs Pakistan	20	6	74.50	2/35	--	99.00	4.52
Tests	69	32	55.69	4/63	--	114.88	--
vs Pakistan	18	6	109.00	1/14	--	176.67	--

Born: **September 6, 1968**
Batting style: **Left-handed**
Bowling style: **Slow left-arm orthodox**
Playing years: **1990-2002**

Saeed **Anwar**

Saeed Anwar spoke so little because he loved to let his bat talk. And when it did, it spoke beautifully and stylishly. He was a lord on the off side. With the cover drive on the up and the square drive being his trademarks, Anwar was also punitive with the hook and pull. As an opening bat, Anwar was often responsible for giving his team an electrifying start. But he was also capable of staying at the wicket for long periods of time. That his two most effective performances came against India proved how much he loved pressure. His 194 in Chennai was a classic example of killing-me-softly for his first 100 runs and then going all out. Anil Kumble in particular will remember an over where Anwar slammed him for four sixes. That the knock came in the Independence Cup in India and that it knocked India out of the tournament will always be special for him. His innings at the Eden Gardens in Kolkata during the Asian Test Championships was easily his best Test innings. Opening the innings Anwar finished with 188 not out and along with Shoaib Akhtar's incisive pace bowling helped Pakistan win the Test match. A quiet man, Anwar became a devout Muslim after his daughter's death in 2001. He left the stage in style, cracking a masterly 101 against India at Centurion in the World Cup. Sadly for Pakistan, it was a lost cause.

Batting & Fielding	M	Runs	Avg	H.S.	100	50	S.R.	Ct
ODIs	247	8823	39.21	194	20	43	80.58	42
vs India	50	2002	43.52	194	4	8	90.71	12
Tests	55	4052	45.53	188*	11	25	--	18
vs India	3	289	57.80	188*	1	1	--	--

Bowling	M	Wkts	Avg	Best	5WI	S.R.	E.R.
ODIs	247	6	31.83	2/9	--	40.33	4.74
vs India	50	--	--	0/2	--	--	3.00
Tests	55	--	--	0/0	--	--	--
vs India	3	--	--	--	--	--	--

Asif Iqbal

Born: **June 6, 1943**
Batting style: **Right-handed**
Bowling style: **Right-arm medium**
Playing years: **1964-1980**

Born in Hyderabad, India, Asif Iqbal (a nephew of former India off-spinner and BCCI president Ghulam Ahmed), migrated to Pakistan in the 60s. He was a fine batsman and a hare between the wickets. In 58 Tests matches he scored 3575 runs. Asif is remembered for a record ninth-wicket stand with Intikhab Alam. He led Pakistan to two World Cups in 1975 and 1979. When India toured Pakistan in 1978 he batted at No. 6 and scored 104 in the second innings of the first Test and 44 in the third when promoted to five. When Pakistan came to India the next year, he was the unanimous choice as captain. Pakistan was trying to buy ground with his Indian lineage. It didn't work though, as Pakistan lost 0-2, and Asif himself had a poor series. A 55 in the first Test, 64 and 38 in the second was all that he had to show as our Pakistani ran into Haryana Hurricane, Kapil Dev. Asif was alleged to have allowed India to bat first 'fixing' the toss in the Calcutta Test. He joined the CBFS (Cricketers Benefit Fund Series) in Sharjah and was responsible for players earning fat cheques through the benefit series. He played with distinction for Kent in county cricket.

Batting & Fielding	M	Runs	Avg	H.S.	100	50	S.R.	Ct
ODIs	10	330	55.00	52	--	5	70.66	7
vs India	1	62	62.00	62	--	1	86.11	--
Tests	58	3575	38.86	175	11	12	--	36
vs India	9	466	33.29	104	1	2	--	5

Bowling	M	Wkts	Avg	Best	5WI	S.R.	E.R.
ODIs	10	16	23.63	4/56	--	37.00	3.83
vs India	1	1	44.00	1/44	--	48.00	5.50
Tests	58	53	28.34	5/48	2	72.91	--
vs India	9	2	36.00	1/3	--	109.00	--

Born: **February 8, 1963**
Batting style: **Right-handed**
Bowling style: **Right-arm slow**
Playing years: **1984-2000**

Mohammed **Azharuddin**

So often is the word tragic used in modern day sport, that it almost amounts to abuse. But Mohammed Azharuddin was the quintessential tragic hero of Indian and international cricket. Sample this: highest score of 199; finished his career at 99 Tests; scored countless runs at his beloved Eden Gardens, but failed to get off the mark in that World Cup semifinal against Sri Lanka in 1996, and was booed by the fans who thought he was God; and of course, the match-fixing allegations. He will always be the original wunderkind of Indian cricket after his three successive 100s in his first three Tests against England. A stylist to the core, Azhar played with magical wrists and is also the only cricketer to have scored a 100 in his first and last Test. He was also responsible for building the team of the 90s and emerged as an astute captain who made India almost unbeatable at home. Azhar scored three 100s against Pakistan in Tests with his highest being 141 at Kolkata in 1987-87. Though, for sheer drama, his 109 in the second Test in Faisalabad in 1989-90 takes the prize as it helped save India the Test match. His ODI record against Pakistan is modest but he will always be remembered as the captain who led India to three victories in World Cup matches against them.

Batting & Fielding	M	Runs	Avg	H.S.	100	50	S.R.	Ct
ODIs	334	9378	36.92	153*	7	58	73.94	156
vs Pakistan	64	1657	31.87	101	2	9	67.72	44
Tests	99	6215	45.04	199	22	21	--	105
vs Pakistan	12	769	40.47	141	3	3	--	14

Bowling	M	Wkts	Avg	Best	5WI	S.R.	E.R.
ODIs	334	12	40.08	3/19	--	46.33	5.19
vs Pakistan	64	--	--	0/6	--	--	6.65
Tests	99	--	--	0/4	--	--	--
vs Pakistan	12	--	--	--	--	--	--

Born: **September 25, 1946**
Batting style: **Right-handed**
Bowling style: **Slow left-arm orthodox**
Playing years: **1966-1979**

No left-arm spinner attracted so much attention as this Sikh from Amritsar. With languid action he mesmerized the batsmen with control of length and direction and variation of flight. Bishen Singh Bedi's bowling was described as poetry in motion. He had a strong wrist and could get the arm-ball to really whiz into the unsuspecting batsman. He catapulted into the Test arena following a fine performance for the Universities against West Indies in 1966. Incidentally, the first Test he watched was the one he played in, against the West Indies at Kolkata in 1966-67. In 67 Tests he accounted for 266 batsmen (average 28.71). Bedi was the first Indian to cross the landmark of 200 Test wickets. He led India in 22 matches. His best was 7 for 98 in the fourth Test against Australia in 1969-70, and 10 for 194 in the second Test against the Australians at Perth in 1977. Against Pakistan in 1978-79, Bedi didn't perform to his full potential, claiming just 6 wickets in the three Tests. Bedi was indeed a good ambassador of cricket as he proved while leading the team in this path-breaking tour. The series also marked the end of the glorious spin era.

Batting & Fielding	M	Runs	Avg	H.S.	100	50	S.R.	Ct
ODIs	10	31	6.20	13	--	--	51.67	4
vs Pakistan	3	2	2.00	2	--	--	20.00	1
Tests	67	656	8.99	50*	--	1	--	26
vs Pakistan	3	10	2.50	4	--	--	--	1

Bowling	M	Wkts	Avg	Best	5WI	S.R.	E.R.
ODIs	10	7	48.57	2/44	--	84.29	3.46
vs Pakistan	3	2	50.00	2/44	--	54.00	5.56
Tests	67	266	28.71	7/98	14	80.32	--
vs Pakistan	3	6	74.83	3/124	--	138.00	--

Bishen Singh Bedi

Ramakant **Desai**

Born: **July 20, 1939**
Batting style: **Right-handed**
Bowling style: **Right-arm medium pace**
Playing years: **1958-1968**

No Indian opening bowler made such an impact in a home series as Ramakant Desai. Just a slip of a man, he claimed five wickets for a CCI side against West Indies in 1958-59 and earned his national cap against them the same year. He went on to capture 50 wickets in his first Ranji season. Desai also claimed the quickest 100 in Ranji trophy in 471.5 overs. In 28 Tests, he captured 74 wickets. Of these, 21 came against Pakistan. In particular, Hanif Mohammad became his rival, and he would inevitably get him out. In the 1960 series, Mohammed made 160 in the first innings of the Bombay Test, but was out for a duck in the second innings caught by Umrigar off Desai with whom he helped plan the dismissals. Desai had the Pakistani rival again at Calcutta and in both innings of the last Test at Delhi when he claimed eight wickets in the match. In that series Desai also scored his highest, an 85 adding 149 for the ninth wicket with Nana Joshi in the Bombay Test. Past his prime, Desai was picked for the 1967-68 tours of Australia and New Zealand. He did well in the latter tour. On retirement he became national selector and manager of Mumbai Ranji trophy teams before an untimely death a few years ago.

Batting & Fielding	M	Runs	Avg	H.S.	100	50	S.R.	Ct
ODIs	Did not play							
vs Pakistan	Did not play							
Tests	28	418	13.48	85	--	1	--	9
vs Pakistan	5	134	26.80	85	--	1	--	1

Bowling	M	Wkts	Avg	Best	5WI	S.R.	E.R.
ODIs	Did not play						
vs Pakistan	Did not play						
Tests	28	74	37.31	6/56	2	75.64	--
vs Pakistan	5	21	29.76	4/66	--	61.67	--

Born: **January 1, 1973**
Batting style: **Right-handed**
Bowling style: **Right-arm**
Playing years: **1996-**

Rahul **Dravid**

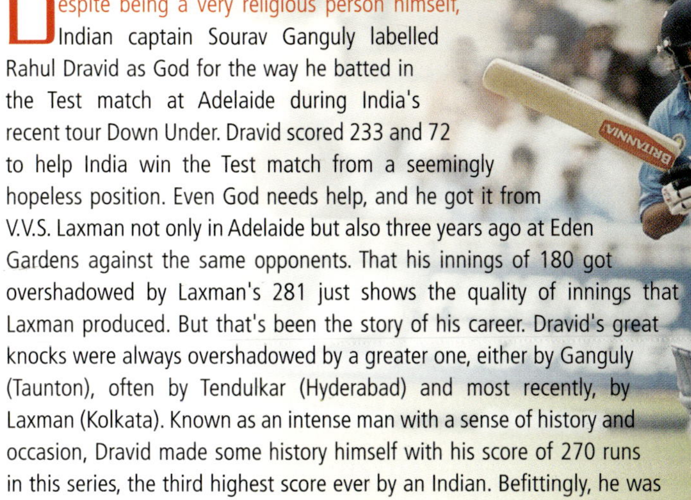

Despite being a very religious person himself, Indian captain Sourav Ganguly labelled Rahul Dravid as God for the way he batted in the Test match at Adelaide during India's recent tour Down Under. Dravid scored 233 and 72 to help India win the Test match from a seemingly hopeless position. Even God needs help, and he got it from V.V.S. Laxman not only in Adelaide but also three years ago at Eden Gardens against the same opponents. That his innings of 180 got overshadowed by Laxman's 281 just shows the quality of innings that Laxman produced. But that's been the story of his career. Dravid's great knocks were always overshadowed by a greater one, either by Ganguly (Taunton), often by Tendulkar (Hyderabad) and most recently, by Laxman (Kolkata). Known as an intense man with a sense of history and occasion, Dravid made some history himself with his score of 270 runs in this series, the third highest score ever by an Indian. Befittingly, he was declared Man of the Match.

Batting & Fielding	M	Runs	Avg	H.S.	100	50	S.R.	Ct
ODIs	229	7250	39.40	153	8	51	69.22	134
vs Pakistan	40	1110	32.65	107	1	6	62.71	19
Tests	76	6552	56.97	233	16	32	--	96
vs Pakistan	4	168	24.00	53	--	1	--	7

Bowling	M	Wkts	Avg	Best	5WI	S.R.	E.R.
ODIs	229	4	42.50	2/43	--	46.50	5.48
vs Pakistan	40	1	21.00	1/21	--	24.00	5.25
Tests	76	1	39.00	1/18	--	120.00	--
vs Pakistan	4	Did not bowl					

Fazal Mahmood

Born: **February 18, 1927**
Batting style: **Right-handed**
Bowling style: **Right-arm fast medium**
Playing years: **1952-1962**

Master of the swing and cut, this debonair quick bowler was said to be a combination of England's Alec Besder and West Indian Sonny Ramadhin. He could make the ball talk on matting tracks. In 34 Tests he scored 620 runs and claimed 139 wickets, the best show being sending England hurtling to defeat on home ground in 1952. Like Kardar, Fazal Mahmood too could have played for both India and Pakistan but turned down the Indian tour of Australia in 1948-49. He bowled first change in the first Test at Delhi in 1952 and claimed two wickets, of Lala Amarnath and G.S. Ramchand, plus scoring crucial 20s in both innings at No 7. In the next Test when India provided jute matting instead of coir (which was Fazal's favourite), he claimed 5 for 52 and 7 for 42 leading India to their doom at Lucknow by an innings and 43 runs. He didn't get many wickets later but continued to be handy with the bat. When India toured Pakistan he went wicketless in the first Test but after a moderate return claimed five in the Karachi game. He created diplomatic problems by marking the pitch with a pencil in one Test match in India. Pakistanis suspected that Vizzy, the BCCI president, was watering the pitch at night to help India's cause. In the 1959-60 series Fazal shone in the third Test claiming five wickets and three in the fifth.

Batting & Fielding	M	Runs	Avg	H.S.	100	50	S.R.	Ct
ODIs	Did not Play							
vs India	Did not Play							
Tests	34	620	14.09	60	--	1	--	11
vs India	14	272	17.00	33	--	--	--	5

Bowling	M	Wkts	Avg	Best	5WI	S.R.	E.R.
ODIs	Did not Play						
vs India	Did not Play						
Tests	34	139	24.71	7/42	13	70.75	--
vs India	14	44	24.55	7/42	4	82.61	--

Born: **July 8, 1972**
Batting style: **Left-handed**
Bowling style: **Right-arm medium**
Playing years: **1996-**

Sourav **Ganguly**

MOM is Ganguly's favourite phrase. No, it's not the many Man-of-the-Match trophies he has collected that we are talking about here. It's mind over matter. From being labelled as a guy with a bad attitude and banished from the Indian squad after India's tour to Australia in 1991-92, to being India's most successful captain is an amazing metamorphosis. A century on Test debut at Lords and another one in Trent bridge in the next Test are now part of folklore, as is his keeping Australian captain Steve Waugh waiting for the toss which psyched the Aussies into defeat during their Indian sojourn in 2001. 'The Prince of Kolkata' is truly the King of India today. He led India to the World Cup final, and almost won the Test series Down Unde. Ganguly the captain, is still a major force with the bat, particularly in one-dayers. Pakistan seems to be his favourite opponent, especially in ODIs with the bat and ball. His 124 at Dhaka helped India chase down 316 in 48 overs to lift the Independence Cup and his 141 in Adelaide helped India to get their only victory during their disastrous Australian campaign in 1999-2000. But his greatest exploits came in the Sahara Cup in 1997 where he tormented them with both bat and ball and emerged as the Man-of-the-Series. His 5 for 16 in the third match of the series when Pakistan was chasing 181 for victory helped India win the series 3-0.

Batting & Fielding	M	Runs	Avg	H.S.	100	50	S.R.	Ct
ODIs	249	9309	42.12	183	22	53	75.03	86
vs Pakistan	41	1420	40.57	141	2	9	71.64	11
Tests	72	4509	41.75	173	11	21	--	52
vs Pakistan	3	172	34.40	62*	--	2	--	3

Bowling	M	Wkts	Avg	Best	5WI	S.R.	E.R.
ODIs	249	93	35.14	5/16	2	41.95	5.03
vs Pakistan	41	28	25.64	5/16	1	33.46	4.60
Tests	72	23	50.52	3/28	--	90.09	--
vs Pakistan	3	--	--	0/9	--	--	--

Born: **July 10, 1949**

Batting style: **Right-handed**

Bowling style: **Right-arm medium pace**

Playing years: **1970-1987**

Sunil **Gavaskar**

Famous US hurdler Edwin Moses was once described as the poet-laureate of motion. His equivalent in cricket would be Sunil Gavaskar. At a time when the world of cricket was brimming with fast bowlers like Andy Roberts, Michael Holding, Jeff Thomson, Dennis Lillee and others, Gavaskar stood tall compiling countless runs with a passion. In 1970-71 he made a glorious debut in the West Indies and seven years later, Gavaskar was in full bloom while facing Imran Khan, Sarfraz Nawaz and company. Runs came easily and his prowess reached a zenith in the third Test at Karachi when he got a century in each innings (111 and 137). He got five centuries against Pakistan in all. When Pakistan toured India in 1979, Gavaskar conceived of a wonderful plan. Before, and a few days after Asif Iqbal's team arrived, he praised them saying India stood no chance against the likes of Zaheer Abbas, Imran Khan and the others. The result: The Pakistanis overestimated their own abilities and buckled under a rampaging Kapil Dev. From all of Gavaskar's knocks, the best that will be remembered is the 96 on a minefield of a Bangalore track. India lost that Test in 1986-87. It was also Sunny Gavaskar's swansong.

Batting & Fielding	M	Runs	Avg	H.S.	100	50	S.R.	Ct
ODIs	108	3092	35.14	103*	1	27	62.28	22
vs Pakistan	20	600	33.33	92	--	6	63.90	7
Tests	125	10122	51.12	236*	34	45	--	108
vs Pakistan	24	2089	56.46	166	5	12	--	19

Bowling	M	Wkts	Avg	Best	5WI	S.R.	E.R.
ODIs	108	1	25.00	1/10	--	20.00	7.50
vs Pakistan	20	1	14.00	1/10	--	11.00	7.64
Tests	125	1	206.00	1/34	--	380.00	--
vs Pakistan	24	1	84.00	1/34	--	120.00	--

Hanif Mohammad

Born: **December 21, 1924**
Batting style: **Right-handed**
Bowling style: **Right-arm off break**
Playing years: **1952-1970**

From the famous family of five brothers, four of whom played Test cricket, Hanif ranks among the world's great opening batsmen. Famous for his triple hundred against West Indies, Hanif ended up with 3915 runs from 55 Tests for an average of 43 plus. Hanif was just 17 on his maiden tour to India in 1952. He feasted on Indian bowling. In the first Test at Delhi he scored 51 and 34, 96 in the second and 56 in the fifth. He scored 917 runs for an average of 65 on that tour. When India toured Pakistan he scored 41 at Dhaka, 142 at Bahawalpur but faded away after that. Back in India in 1959-60, he began with a 160 at the Brabourne Stadium, followed by a duck against Ramakant Desai, who was to be his bugbear. He had two 50s in the Calcutta Test and 62 at Madras but was claimed by Desai in both innings of the final Test at Delhi.

Batting & Fielding	M	Runs	Avg	H.S.	100	50	S.R.	Ct
ODIs	Did not Play							
vs India	Did not Play							
Tests	55	3915	43.99	337	12	15	--	40
vs India	15	970	40.42	160	2	6	--	5

Bowling	M	Wkts	Avg	Best	5WI	S.R.	E.R.
ODIs	Did not Play						
vs India	Did not Play						
Tests	55	1	95.00	1/1	--	206.00	--
vs India	15	1	59.00	1/34	--	126.00	--

Born: **September 20, 1968**
Batting style: **Right-handed**
Bowling style: **Left-arm medium**
Playing years: **1986-2001**

Ijaz Ahmed

This middle-order batsman can be best described in one simple word: flamboyant. There was an air of cockiness in his walk that he translated into runs. Indians would recall Lahore in 1997. Sent in to open the innings, Ijaz slammed 134 off just 84 balls with 10 boundaries and 9 sixes to help Pakistan win in the most convincing fashion. He was not the most attractive batsman to watch. In fact he was rather ungainly. But the methods he affected were extremely successful and it fetched him runs. Ijaz, a willing bat at No. 3 was a decent all rounder and could bowl medium pace as well as left-arm spin, though he was a right-hand bat. Ijaz played only four Tests against India and did not do too well. He had a highly successful ODI career.

Batting & Fielding	M	Runs	Avg	H.S.	100	50	S.R.	Ct
ODIs	250	6564	32.33	139*	10	37	80.20	90
vs India	53	1533	35.65	139*	2	6	79.22	20
Tests	60	3315	37.67	211	12	12	--	45
vs India	4	56	8.00	17	--	--	--	6

Bowling	M	Wkts	Avg	Best	5WI	S.R.	E.R.
ODIs	250	5	95.20	2/31	--	127.40	4.48
vs India	53	--	--	0/10	--	--	3.89
Tests	60	2	38.50	1/9	--	90.00	--
vs India	Did not bowl						

Born: **November 25, 1952**
Batting style: **Right-handed**
Bowling style: **Right-arm fast**
Playing years: **1971-1992**

Imran Khan

What did he break more, batsmen's knuckles with his searing pace or the hearts of millions of female fans the world over with his dapper looks? Either way, it was a good contest because he did both in style. Imran Khan was, is and forever will be the uncrowned king of Pakistani cricket. He had everything going for him: a Cambridge degree, royal blood and unsurpassed talent. He was a born leader and did the most difficult job of leading a talented side of individuals with egos the size of elephants. A fantastic motivator, Imran was the man who made the Pakistanis believe in themselves, especially in the 1992 World Cup where they were one match away from elimination and ended up as champions. His performance against India was brilliant. He picked up 94 wickets in 23 Tests; he played against the arch-rivals at a bowling average of 24.04 with six five-wicket hauls. He was unbelievable in the 1982-83 series as he bowled with a stress fracture of the shin and yet picked up 40 wickets. His second innings spell of 8-60 in the second Karachi Test where he also got his 200th Test wicket was nothing short of extraordinary. Imran himself rates the second spell where he took 5 for 3 in 25 balls as the fastest he's ever bowled. One of the pioneers of reverse swing, Imran was responsible for grooming and passing on the tricks of the trade to youngsters like Waqar Younis, Wasim Akram and others.

Batting & Fielding	M	Runs	Avg	H.S.	100	50	S.R.	Ct
ODIs	175	3709	33.41	102*	1	19	72.67	37
vs India	29	433	21.65	73	--	1	79.89	7
Tests	88	3807	37.69	136	6	18	--	28
vs India	23	1091	51.95	135*	3	3	--	7

Bowling	M	Wkts	Avg	Best	5WI	S.R.	E.R.
ODIs	175	182	26.62	6/14	1	41.00	3.90
vs India	29	35	22.29	6/14	1	34.66	3.86
Tests	88	362	22.81	8/58	23	53.75	--
vs India	23	94	24.04	8/60	6	54.02	--

Inzamam-ul-Haq

Born: **March 3, 1970**
Batting style: **Right-handed**
Bowling style: **Slow left-arm**
Playing years: **1992-**

There is such an air of casualness to Inzamam, or Inzy, that it is difficult to imagine that he can play all those shots with authority and seriousness. He entered the world cricket arena in the most destructive fashion. Inzy powered a quick half-century at more than two runs a ball to help Pakistan beat New Zealand in the semi-finals of the 1992 World Cup. Pakistan, with Imran Khan in the saddle went on to win the title. He is powerfully built and that reflects in his shots. The Indians have been at the receiving end in the recent ODI series. There is a subtlety in his knocks, and it is no surprise that Imran rates him as one of the best players of fast bowling. Anybody who has a triple century in Tests is a world-class batsman and so is Inzy. His rotund figure – Inzy has been harangued with 'aloo' (potato) from the stands – has caused Inzy immense problems, especially running between the wickets. His partner is always under threat. During the Sahara Cup series a few years ago, Inzy threatened a spectator who was overdoing the aloo business. But Inzy shed some weight post-World Cup, where he was not in the best of forms, and has shown the ability to don the thinking cap as the captain. The Indo-Pak series is the real challenge. He has so far played in two Tests against India.

Batting & Fielding	M	Runs	Avg	H.S.	100	50	S.R.	Ct
ODIs	312	9796	39.18	137*	10	68	73.04	94
vs India	50	1795	44.88	123	4	8	78.11	19
Tests	92	6757	49.68	329	18	36	--	70
vs India	3	170	28.33	77	--	2	--	2

Bowling	M	Wkts	Avg	Best	5WI	S.R.	E.R.
ODIs	312	3	21.33	1/0	--	19.33	6.62
vs India	50	--	--	0/10	--	--	10.00
Tests	92	--	--	0/8	--	--	--
vs India	Did not bowl						

Born: **January 17, 1925**
Batting style: **Left-handed**
Bowling style: **Left-arm medium pace**
Playing years: **1952-1958 (against India)**

Abdul Hafeez **Kardar**

Kardar played for both India and Pakistan. He toured England with India in 1946 and then led the first Pakistan team that toured India in 1952. An alumnus of Lahore's Islamia College, he was known for his grace as a left-handed slow bowler and for his fast batting. He played for Oxford University. He represented Northern India in the Ranji trophy during the pre-Partition era. Knocks of 143 against Western India and 145 against Bombay in 1944 stand out. He led Pakistan to India in 1952 and notched their first win in Lucknow, thanks to Fazal Mahmood's heroics on a jute matting wicket. In the Madras Test he hit a 79 and had 2 wickets. Emphasis on not losing the home series in 1954-55 meant fewer runs and wickets. He had a knock of 44 and 2 wickets in the third Test before signing off with a 93 in the fifth Test at Karachi. Kardar went on to become an able cricket administrator in Pakistan.

Batting & Fielding	M	Runs	Avg	H.S.	100	50	S.R.	Ct
ODIs	Did not Play							
vs India	Did not Play							
Tests	23	847	24.91	93	--	5	--	15
vs India	10	380	25.33	93	--	2	--	5

Bowling	M	Wkts	Avg	Best	5WI	S.R.	E.R.
ODIs	Did not Play						
vs India	Did not Play						
Tests	23	21	45.43	3/35	--	129.14	--
vs India	10	8	37.00	2/20	--	114.75	--

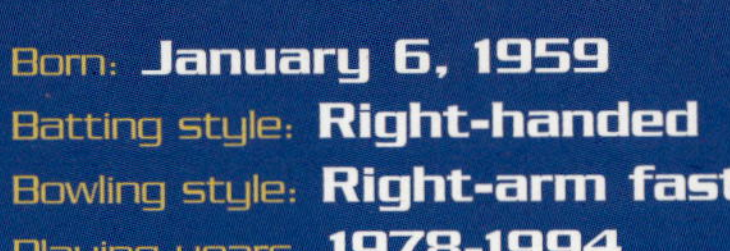

Born: **January 6, 1959**
Batting style: **Right-handed**
Bowling style: **Right-arm fast**
Playing years: **1978-1994**

If Mohinder Amarnath loved Pakistani bowling, Kapil Dev loved their batsmen. In 29 Tests, the Haryana Hurricane had 99 Pakistani scalps with 8 for 85 at his best. Strangely, batting was a letdown, just 1054 runs with 84 as his highest. Kapil's arrival in 1978-79 heralded two major things: India had at last found a fast bowler with a large heart and also the decline of the spin quartet. Three Tests and seven wickets gave him a quiet entry into Test cricket. But Pakistan found him to be a handful while touring India the next year and in the home series in 1982-83. Six Tests in the 1979-80 series saw Kapil Dev claiming 32 wickets on home pitches. On the 1982-83 tour, he was almost a match for Imran Khan and Co. with 24 wickets. In the third Test at Faisalabad, Pakistan ran up 652 with four making centuries. Kapil had 7-220. In the fifth Test at Lahore, Pakistan were 'bowled out' for 323 with Kapil claiming 8-85. If only he had some support from the other end!

Batting & Fielding	M	Runs	Avg	H.S.	100	50	S.R.	Ct
ODIs	225	3782	23.79	175*	1	14	94.41	71
vs Pakistan	32	382	15.28	59	--	1	92.27	9
Tests	131	5248	31.05	163	8	27	--	64
vs Pakistan	29	1054	27.03	84	--	8	--	9

Bowling	M	Wkts	Avg	Best	5WI	S.R.	E.R.
ODIs	225	253	27.45	5/43	1	44.28	3.72
vs Pakistan	32	42	26.50	3/17	--	37.74	4.21
Tests	131	434	29.65	9/83	23	63.92	--
vs Pakistan	29	99	30.12	8/85	7	60.04	50.17

BNZ
NZ

Anil **Kumble**

Born: **October 17, 1970**
Batting style: **Right-handed**
Bowling style: **Right-arm leg break**
Playing years: **1990-**

Anil Kumble has been such a giant in Indian cricket that his achievements have made every critic of his feel small. Be it Azhar, Tendulkar or Ganguly, captains have searched for him in the field frantically whenever they have needed a wicket or needed to stop runs. And he has always stepped in and delivered the goods with great calmness. When Pakistan was making a mockery of a stiff Indian target in that World Cup quarter-final in Bangalore, and captain Azharuddin was looking worried, Anil Kumble stepped in and produced a spell of 3 for 48 to help India win. Again, when Pakistan looked like chasing 420 in the Ferozshah Kotla Test in 1999 and were 101 for no loss, Anil Kumble took 10 for 74, making him the second man since England's Jim Laker to take all 10 in an innings. His recent performance in Australia where he took 24 wickets proved all critics, who said he is ineffective on true pitches, wrong. Indian supporters prayed that Kumble would make a comeback from injury and bowl India to their first Test win in Pakistan. Not only were their prayers answered, Kumble became the highest wicket-taker in the series with 15 wickets and the Golden Ball to his credit.

Batting & Fielding	M	Runs	Avg	H.S.	100	50	S.R.	Ct
ODIs	251	867	10.45	26	--	--	62.11	83
vs Pakistan	31	155	10.33	16	--	--	64.05	14
Tests	82	1408	16.76	88	--	3	--	37
vs Pakistan	4	54	9.00	18	--	--	--	3

Bowling	M	Wkts	Avg	Best	5WI	S.R.	E.R.
ODIs	251	315	30.25	6/12	2	42.60	4.26
vs Pakistan	31	49	23.98	4/12	--	34.12	4.22
Tests	82	390	28.16	10/74	24	67.40	--
Pakistan	4	30	20.77	10/74	3	42.73	--

Born: **September 11, 1911**
Batting style: **Right-handed**
Bowling style: **Right-arm medium pace**
Playing years: **1933-1953**

Lala Amarnath

This proud Punjabi was an all-rounder in the truest sense: a mid-order batsman, a useful swing and cut bowler, and also a capable wicketkeeper. Unfortunately, his performance of 878 runs from 28 Tests (average 24.38) and 45 wickets (average 32.91) did not match his ability. His 5-118 performance at Lord's in 1946 when he sent back batsmen Len Hutton, Denis Compton, Cyril Washbrook, Wally Hammond and Joe Hardstaff was unforgettable. Amarnath led India in the first series against Pakistan, scoring 61 in the second Test at Lucknow, which Pakistan won by an innings. He claimed four wickets in the ten-wicket win over Pakistan at Bombay. He led India brilliantly in Australia 1948-49 matching wits with the great Sir Don Bradman. Lala's contemporaries freely use the words belligerent, original, unpredictable, outspoken, and genius to describe him. On retirement he became an able coach, manager, selector and commentator. He had three sons, two of whom, Surinder and Mohinder, played for India.

Batting & Fielding	M	Runs	Avg	H.S.	100	50	S.R.	Ct
ODIs	Did not play							
vs Pakistan	Did not play							
Tests	24	878	24.39	118	1	4	--	13
vs Pakistan	5	105	26.25	61*	--	1	--	2

Bowling	M	Wkts	Avg	Best	5WI	S.R.	E.R.
ODIs	Did not play						
vs Pakistan	Did not play						
Tests	24	45	32.91	5/96	2	94.24	--
vs Pakistan	5	9	22.44	4/40	--	85.22	--

Sanjay **Manjrekar**

Born: **July 12, 1965**
Batting style: **Right-handed**
Bowling style: **Right-arm leg break**
Playing years: **1987-1997**

Sanjay Manjrekar made everybody notice his talent during India's disastrous sojourn to the West Indies in 1989. Handling the pace quarter of Marshall, Bishop, Walsh and Ambrose with élan, he scored a scintillating 100 in Barbados. But his really big performance came in Pakistan in 1989 when he scored 569 runs in four Tests with two 100s. His 218 at Lahore remains the highest Test score by an Indian against Pakistan. Manjrekar was also part of the squad when India beat Pakistan in two World Cup matches in 1992 in Sydney and the memorable Bangalore quarter-final in 1996. Sound defence, supreme technique and strokes all around the wicket – there was nothing in the art of batsmanship that he didn't have. But like most technicians he was obsessed with it and often fell slave to his technique. Nevertheless, he did yeoman service to Indian cricket whenever he was selected. He often found himself in and out of the Indian team and sensing that he had little chance of making it back to the squad, he retired in 1997-98.

Batting & Fielding	M	Runs	Avg	H.S.	100	50	S.R.	Ct
ODIs	74	1994	33.23	105	1	15	64.43	23
vs Pakistan	13	367	33.36	72	--	4	69.51	2
Tests	37	2043	37.15	218	4	9	--	25
vs Pakistan	4	569	94.83	218	2	3	--	3

Bowling	M	Wkts	Avg	Best	5WI	S.R.	E.R.
ODIs	74	1	10.00	1/2	--	8.00	7.50
vs Pakistan	Did not bowl						
Tests	37	--	--	0/4	--	--	--
vs Pakistan	Did not bowl						

Born: **September 26, 1931**
Batting style: **Right-handed**
Bowling style: **Right-arm off break**
Playing years: **1951-1965**

Vijay **Manjrekar**

He is rated as India's all-time great batsman, equally comfortable against both pace and spin. In 55 Tests he scored 3,208 runs (average 39.12). He also kept wickets in one Test. Manjrekar came to the fore when still in school and cemented his place in the Indian middle order from the 50s to the 60s. Manjrekar's specialty was the cut off the back foot, shortening the length of the ball. His century against England at Leeds is one of the finest batting feats of Indian cricket. Coming when three wickets were down, Manjrekar batted with such ease and expertise that a senior player, Vijay Hazare was inspired to play well and get a 100. Manjrekar had two 50s in the first Test against Pakistan at Dhaka in 1954-55. When Pakistan visited India he was prolific at the start of the series. Manjrekar's son Sanjay, too, played for India.

Batting & Fielding	M	Runs	Avg	H.S.	100	50	S.R.	Ct
ODIs	Did not play							
vs Pakistan	Did not play							
Tests	55	3208	39.12	189*	7	15	--	19
vs Pakistan	13	574	38.27	74*	--	5	--	2

Bowling	M	Wkts	Avg	Best	5WI	S.R.	E.R.
ODIs	Did not play						
vs Pakistan	Did not play						
Tests	55	1	44.00	1/16	--	204.00	--
vs Pakistan	13	--	--	0/2	--	--	--

Miandad Javed

Born: **June 12, 1957**
Batting style: **Right-handed**
Bowling style: **Right-arm leg break**
Playing years: **1976-1994**

He sledged, he ran the fielders ragged, and he was not the prettiest batsman to watch. But when it came to playing for Pakistan he had a real talent. Miandad loved a scrap and his combative instincts often got him under the skin of his opponents. Ask Dennis Lillie, who was beaten at his trade, by Javed in Perth in 1983-84. Miandad brought out all his fighting qualities against India and his record is outstanding. In 28 Tests he scored 2228 runs at an average of 67.51 runs (a good 15 points higher than his career average) with five 100s and fourteen 50s. His highest score of 280 not out came in Hyderabad (Sind) in 1982-83 where, along with Mudassar Nazar, Miandad added 451 runs for the third wicket which helped Pakistan beat India by an innings. His performance in ODIs against India is no different. In 35 matches he scored 1175 runs at an average of 51.08 (nine points higher than his career average) with three 100s and six 50s. His most memorable innings of course was his unbeaten 116 in the Australasia Cup final in Sharjah. The last ball six which he hit off Chetan Sharma will always be etched in the minds of the supporters of both countries. He played a key role in Pakistan winning the World Cup in 1992. He was also captain of the Pakistan team but his aggressive nature often led him to fall out with the players.

Batting & Fielding	M	Runs	Avg	H.S.	100	50	S.R.	Ct
ODIs	233	7381	41.70	119*	8	50	66.94	72
vs India	35	1175	51.09	119*	3	6	72.17	13
Tests	124	8832	52.57	280*	23	43	--	93
vs India	28	2228	67.52	280*	5	14	--	18

Bowling	M	Wkts	Avg	Best	5WI	S.R.	E.R.
ODIs	233	7	42.43	2/22	--	62.29	4.09
vs India	Did not bowl						
Tests	124	17	40.12	3/74	--	86.47	--
vs India	28	1	42.00	1/7	--	84.00	--

Born: **April 12, 1917**
Batting style: **Right-handed**
Bowling style: **Left-arm orthodox**
Playing years: **1946-1959**

Vinoo Mankad

He was India's greatest all-rounder. A right-hand opening batsman and left-arm spinner, Mankad was a Trojan for work. In 44 Tests he hit 2,109 runs and claimed 162 wickets. He achieved the quickest double, 1,000 runs and 100 wickets in Tests in his 23rd and was the first post-war visiting bowler to the double on an England tour. Two performances stand out – his century against Lindwall and Miller and eight wickets that shaped India's win over Australia in Madras in 1946-47. Then, of course, the Mankad Test at Lord's in 1952 when he scored 74 and 184 and claimed five for 196 in 73 overs. Pakistan suffered, too, Mankad claiming 8-52 and 5-79 as India beat them by innings and 70 in the Delhi Test. He was also a member of the 1955 team that toured Pakistan. Mankad's best performance came in the fourth Test at Peshawar when he claimed 5 for 64 in the second innings. A fearless batsman, Mankad seldom hit recklessly and his five 100s and two double 100s came as an opener. Mankad was a much sought-after professional in the Lancashire league, and also in India, where he played for half a dozen first-class sides. On retirement he turned into a great coach. Of his three sons, Ashok played for India and the other two Atul and Rahul played first-class cricket.

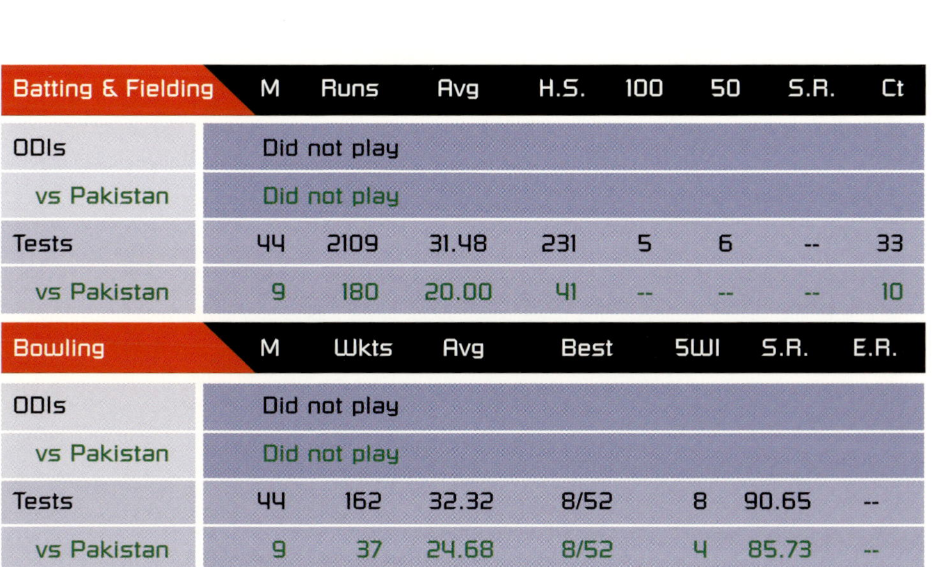

Batting & Fielding	M	Runs	Avg	H.S.	100	50	S.R.	Ct
ODIs	Did not play							
vs Pakistan	Did not play							
Tests	44	2109	31.48	231	5	6	--	33
vs Pakistan	9	180	20.00	41	--	--	--	10

Bowling	M	Wkts	Avg	Best	5WI	S.R.	E.R.
ODIs	Did not play						
vs Pakistan	Did not play						
Tests	44	162	32.32	8/52	8	90.65	--
vs Pakistan	9	37	24.68	8/52	4	85.73	--

Born: **September 23, 1971**
Batting style: **Right-handed**
Bowling style: **Wicket-keeper**
Playing years: **1990-**

Moin Khan

One can expect two things from Moin Khan: shouts of `well bowled' and 'shabbash' (well done), and a quick knock. Moin has an Aristotlean look on his face. He briefly led Pakistan but bickering within the team saw Moin getting only a short term. Moin was not in the best of form against the Indians in the ODI series. But one can never say when he will strike again. The dapper wicket keeper uses his bat like a scimitar and is capable of turning an ODI match on its head. In fact, the Indians need to be wary of his prowess in matches to come. Moin has struggled to keep his place in the Pakistan team. Not the best of keepers, Moin has managed to be ahead of Rashid Latif, who is a better keeper, because of his batting abilities. He is the ideal crisis man for Pakistan. Without being spectacular, Moin improvises in ODIs and that has often helped Pakistan get through tight situations. Moin has played three Tests against India for a tally of 158 runs and has a highest score of 70.

Batting & Fielding	M	Runs	Avg	H.S.	100	50	S.R.	Ct
ODIs	205	3171	23.66	72*	--	12	81.66	203
vs India	46	737	26.32	72	--	3	80.28	53
Tests	68	2735	29.10	137	4	15	--	124
vs India	4	180	22.50	70	--	2	--	5

Bowling	M	Wkts	Avg	Best	5WI	S.R.	E.R.
ODIs	205	Did not bowl					
vs India	46	Did not bowl					
Tests	68	Did not bowl					
vs India	4	Did not bowl					

Mushtaq Mohammed

Born: **November 22, 1943**
Batting style: **Right-handed**
Bowling style: **Right-arm leg break**
Playing years: **1958-1979**

Mushtaq Mohammad became, at 17 years and 78 days, the youngest cricketer to score a Test hundred when he toured India in 1959-60. The third of the famous Mohammad brothers was claimed leg before wicket in both innings in the first Test in the series. He hit 61 when promoted from No. 7 to 6 at Calcutta. He had a 41 at Madras and rose to glory with a 101 in the fifth at Chennai. Mushtaq was around when cricketing ties were restored in 1978 and led a star-studded team. He hit 67 in the second Test and 78 in the third. When he led Pakistan to victory, he didn't endear himself to Indian fans by saying that he hoped Muslims all over the world would savour the win. In a career spanning two decades he scored 3643 runs in 57 Tests and claimed 79 wickets. He played county cricket for Northamptonshire alongside Bishen Singh Bedi. Mushtaq later became the coach for the Pakistani team.

Batting & Fielding	M	Runs	Avg	H.S.	100	50	S.R.	Ct
ODIs	10	209	34.83	55	--	1	59.38	3
vs India	3	22	22.00	16*	--	--	73.33	1
Tests	57	3643	39.17	201	10	19	--	42
vs India	8	413	45.89	101	1	3	--	4

Bowling	M	Wkts	Avg	Best	5WI	S.R.	E.R.
ODIs	10	--	--	0/7	--	--	3.29
vs India	3	Did not bowl					
Tests	57	79	29.23	5/28	3	66.58	--
vs India	8	6	41.17	4/55	--	81.00	--

Born: **July 14, 1962**
Batting style: **Right-handed**
Bowling style: **Right-arm leg spin**
Playing years: **1983-1997**

Ramiz Raja

An underrated batsman, Ramiz Raja probably never enjoyed the attention or the respect he deserved from the Pakistani fans for his cricketing abilities. His situation is akin to the talented all-rounder Abdul Razzaq in the current Pakistan team. But he was a very good player of fast bowling, and fitted nicely in the opening slot after the vacuum was created when the Mudassar Nazar-Mohsin Khan partnership was over. He raised his game against India and in Tests scored 604 runs in 9 Tests with 114 at Jaipur being his highest score. He also scored a crucial 56 in the fourth Test of the 1989 home series at Sialkot to help Pakistan come closer to the Indian first innings score. Ramiz also captained Pakistan but he never got a decent run as skipper.

Passionate about Pakistani cricket, Ramiz is doing a creditable job as the CEO of the Pakistan Cricket Board. He has also made his mark as a TV commentator and a cricket columnist.

Batting & Fielding	M	Runs	Avg	H.S.	100	50	S.R.	Ct
ODIs	198	5841	32.09	119*	9	31	63.18	33
vs India	29	666	23.79	77	--	4	58.78	1
Tests	57	2833	31.83	122	2	22	--	34
vs India	9	604	43.14	114	1	4	--	7

Bowling	M	Wkts	Avg	Best	5WI	S.R.	E.R.
ODIs	198	--	--	0/10	--	--	10.00
vs India	29	Did not bowl					
Tests	57	Did not bowl					
vs India	9	Did not bowl					

Salim Malik

Born: **April 16, 1963**
Batting style: **Right-handed**
Bowling style: **Right-arm off break**
Playing years: **1981-1999**

It is indeed tragic that the cricketing fraternity today will remember Salim Malik only for his involvement in the match-fixing scandal. But for a large part of the 80s and the mid 90s, Malik was the mainstay in the Pakistani middle order. A wristy player much like former Indian captain Mohammed Azharuddin, Malik was a master at the square-cut and cover drive. His 237 against Australia in Lahore in 1994 is still being discussed as one of the greatest match-saving knocks of all time. That his highest one-day score was just 102 shows the problems of batting in the middle order where either he would end up triumphant, or sacrifice his wicket in pursuit of quick runs. He mastered countering Indian bowlers, especially in one-day cricket, though his Test record against India is modest with an average of 35.25 in 22 games with three 100s and 107 being his highest score. In ODIs against India he will always be remembered for his knock of 72 not out off 36 balls in Kolkata to bring Pakistan an unlikely victory when they were chasing 11 runs an over. He was also useful with the ball and his slow leg-cutters helped Pakistan get a breakthrough. Malik was also a fairly successful skipper and led his side to series wins against Australia, New Zealand and Zimbabwe.

Batting & Fielding	M	Runs	Avg	H.S.	100	50	S.R.	Ct
ODIs	283	7171	32.89	102	5	47	76.37	80
vs India	52	1535	34.11	102	2	8	77.17	12
Tests	103	5768	43.70	237	15	29	--	65
vs India	22	846	35.25	107	3	2	--	17

Bowling	M	Wkts	Avg	Best	5WI	S.R.	E.R.
ODIs	283	89	33.25	5/35	1	39.38	5.07
vs India	52	16	26.94	4/36	--	29.25	5.53
Tests	103	5	82.80	1/3	--	146.80	--
vs India	22	2	8.00	1/6	--	30.00	--

Born: **December 1, 1948**
Batting style: **Right-handed**
Bowling style: **Right-arm fast**
Playing years: **1969-1984**

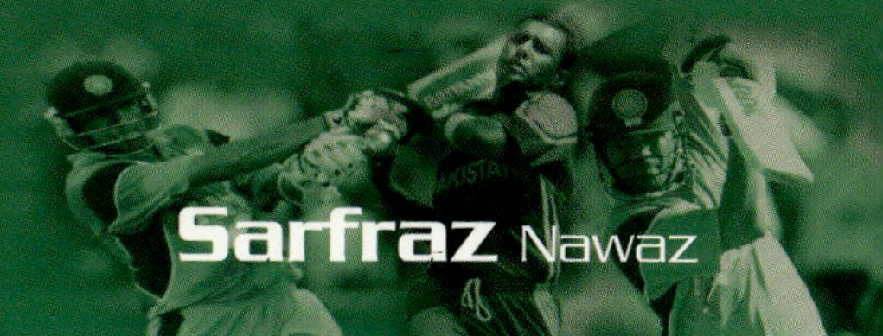

Sarfraz Nawaz

This tall, burly and loud-mouthed Punjabi was an awesome sight. And he was a first-rate bowler. His mouth often got him in the news more than his bowling abilities. Some would disagree of course. Remember Melbourne in 1978-79 when he dismissed seven Aussie batsmen for one run in 33 balls? He finished with nine wickets in that innings. Sarfaraz formed a threatening partnership with Imran Khan. Indeed, when India toured Pakistan in 1978, the duo was at their awesome best. In the third Test at Karachi – the one in which Sunil Gavaskar got two 100s – Sarfraz claimed 9 wickets (4-89 and 5-70). Overall he played four Tests against India and had a rich haul of 36 wickets. Sarfraz's greatest contribution to cricket is the reverse swing. He was accurate and could move the ball both ways. The reverse swing has been passed down generations of Pakistani bowlers and now bowlers all over the world have picked it up too. After retiring Sarfraz became an outspoken Member of Parliament.

Batting & Fielding	M	Runs	Avg	H.S.	100	50	S.R.	Ct
ODIs	45	221	9.61	34*	--	--	63.87	8
vs India	5	18	18.00	14*	--	--	62.07	1
Tests	55	1045	17.71	90	--	4	--	26
vs India	9	113	18.83	28	--	--	--	3

Bowling	M	Wkts	Avg	Best	5WI	S.R.	E.R.
ODIs	45	63	23.22	4/27	--	38.29	3.64
vs India	5	8	15.50	3/31	--	28.50	3.26
Tests	55	177	32.76	9/86	4	78.82	--
vs India	9	36	29.39	5/70	1	64.92	--

Saqlain Mushtaq

Born: **December 29, 1976**
Batting style: **Right-handed**
Bowling style: **Right-arm off break**
Playing years: **1995-**

India must have hoped that this off-spinner would not play in the Test series. Saqlain Mushtaq troubled Indians no end in the 1998-99 series when he claimed 24 wickets in three Tests. In the Chennai Test, made memorable after Sachin Tendulkar scored a magnificent 100, Saqlain claimed 10 wickets as Pakistan won by 12 runs. Saqlain was discovered in 1995-96 during the home series against Sri Lanka, which Pakistan lost. He claimed a wicket off his seventh ball in Tests. Over the years he has improved tremendously and has developed the 'doosra' that turns the other way. Saqlain has bamboozled batsmen with this delivery. He is an excellent ODI bowler as well. Extremely prudent, he has often bowled at the death. He is amongst the few who have taken a hat trick twice in ODIs, both against Zimbabwe. Recently he has shown the ability to bat well too. Coming low down the order, Saqlain can throw his bat around or, as he proved against Zimbabwe in 1996, stay put. Along with Wasim Akram, Saqlain, who also plays for Surrey and has an English wife, holds the world record for the eighth wicket in Tests.

Batting & Fielding	M	Runs	Avg	H.S.	100	50	S.R.	Ct
ODIs	169	709	12.02	37*	--	--	49.96	40
vs India	36	161	16.10	29	--	--	56.89	10
Tests	49	927	14.48	101*	1	2	--	15
vs India	4	34	4.86	21	--	--	--	2

Bowling	M	Wkts	Avg	Best	5WI	S.R.	E.R.
ODIs	169	288	21.79	5/20	6	30.45	4.29
vs India	36	57	24.39	5/45	1	32.35	4.52
Tests	49	208	29.84	8/164	13	67.64	--
vs India	4	25	28.28	5/93	4	55.40	--

Born: **October 20, 1978**

Batting style: **Right-handed**

Bowling style: **Right-arm off break**

Playing years: **2001-**

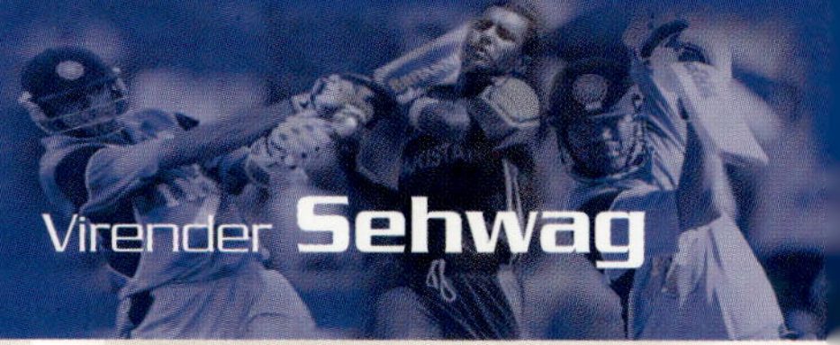

Virender **Sehwag**

Though his career has been brief, Virender Sehwag has achieved immense recognition, the most significant of which elicits comparisons with the great Sachin Tendulkar. But that would be unfair to both him and Tendulkar. His 100 on debut at Bloemfontein was a treat, as were his two 100s on wickets resembling a botanical garden in New Zealand. He is still to play a sizeable number of games against Pakistan but the way he played during his cowboy knock of 79 in Karachi, he will surely leave Pakistan with a lot of fans. His 195 in the Melbourne Test during the recently concluded Test series in Australia showed that Sehwag can play a long innings and can only increase his prominence. A promise fulfilled by his becoming the first Indian to break the 300 barrier with a score of 309 runs in this series. Declared Man of the Series.

Batting & Fielding	M	Runs	Avg	H.S.	100	50	S.R.	Ct
ODIs	90	2819	34.38	130	6	13	96.11	32
vs Pakistan	7	186	26.57	79	--	1	114.11	2
Tests	21	1822	53.59	309	6	5	--	25
vs Pakistan	1	309	309.00	309	1	--	--	1

Bowling	M	Wkts	Avg	Best	5WI	S.R.	E.R.
ODIs	90	41	40.61	3/25	--	45.73	5.33
vs Pakistan	7	2	77.00	1/29	--	66.00	7.00
Tests	21	3	93.67	1/17	--	157.00	--
vs Pakistan	1	--	--	0/18	--	--	--

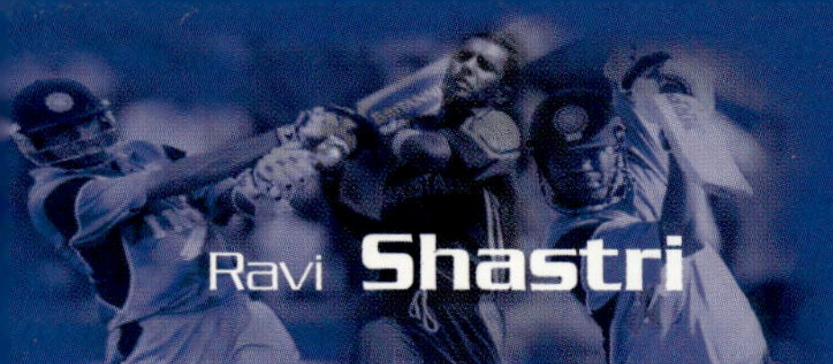

Ravi **Shastri**

Born: **May 27, 1962**
Batting style: **Right-handed**
Bowling style: **Slow left-arm**
Playing years: **1980-1993**

Batting & Fielding	M	Runs	Avg	H.S.	100	50	S.R.	Ct
ODIs	150	3108	29.05	109	4	18	60.51	40
vs Pakistan	29	510	28.33	77	--	5	63.04	12
Tests	80	3830	35.79	206	11	12	--	36
vs Pakistan	15	801	38.14	139	3	3	--	6

Bowling	M	Wkts	Avg	Best	5WI	S.R.	E.R.
ODIs	150	129	36.05	5/15	1	51.26	4.22
vs Pakistan	29	24	39.71	4/38	-	52.58	4.53
Tests	80	151	40.96	5/75	2	104.31	--
vs Pakistan	15	24	46.29	5/75	1	119.17	--

R stands for Ravishankar, R also stands for resilience. Shastri epitomized it. A left-arm trundler who turned into a superb batsman-cum-bowler, the Mumbai cricketer had everything in him – a strong will, fighting qualities and the ability to adapt to any situation. The slam-bang of ODIs and the patience of playing out Test cricket came with a gifted ease to him. He toured Pakistan thrice and struck a century apiece in 1982-83 (128) and 1984-85 (139). Another Test hundred (125) came at Jaipur in 1986-87. What was significant about the three knocks was that the first came as an opener and the next two at No.6 and 7. In 1982-83, he faced Imran Khan at his lethal best, and took on the emerging Wasim Akram in the late 80s and before his premature retirement in the early 90s.

India's tour of Pakistan in 1984-85 was abruptly called off following the assassination of Prime Minister Indira Gandhi. The three-Test series was reduced to two and both were drawn. In a team led by Sunil Gavaskar and containing more established players like Dilip Vengsarkar, Mohinder Amarnath and Sandeep Patil, Shastri was the leading scorer with 210 runs. He also had four wickets in the series with a best of 3 for 90.

Born: **August 13, 1975**
Batting style: **Right-handed**
Bowling style: **Right-arm fast**
Playing years: **1997-**

Shoaib Akhtar

With his mane flying in the air, a long run-up and a flamboyancy that can be associated with fast bowling, Pakistan's Shoaib Akhtar has it all. Hailing from Rawalpindi he earned the alias Rawalpindi Express. He came into the world scene during the 1999 World Cup. At that stage, Shoaib's biggest ambition was to break the speed barrier of 100 mph. So he came fast and faster, and went out even faster with injuries. Twice he was accused of chucking (bowling with a bend-arm action), and both times he was cleared. There were uncertainties around his international future. But Shoaib has hit back powerfully. Shoaib has yet to claim wickets to do justice to his enormous talent. Often he produces that unbeatable delivery. And the Indians, especially Sachin Tendulkar, would recollect the havoc he created in the Kolkata Asian Test championship tie when he picked up four wickets in each innings. That has been his only Test against the Indians. He bowled Tendulkar with a beauty. In the recent ODI series against India, he produced two superb deliveries to get rid of V.V.S. Laxman twice.

Batting & Fielding	M	Runs	Avg	H.S.	100	50	S.R.	Ct
ODIs	103	291	11.64	43	--	--	72.57	14
vs India	19	16	8.00	9*	--	--	42.11	1
Tests	30	250	7.58	37	--	--	--	7
vs India	2	9	2.25	4	--	--	--	--

Bowling	M	Wkts	Avg	Best	5WI	S.R.	E.R.
ODIs	103	167	22.15	6/16	3	29.10	4.57
vs India	19	28	24.71	3/19	--	34.07	4.35
Tests	30	118	24.42	6/11	8	45.18	--
vs India	2	8	29.63	4/47	--	53.63	--

K. Srikkanth

Born: **December 21, 1958**
Batting style: **Right-handed**
Bowling style: **Right-arm off break**
Playing years: **1981-1992**

In a list of immortals like Sunil Gavaskar, Mohinder Amarnath and Gundappa Viswanath, the flamboyant Srikkanth would not even get a footnote – certainly not for his batting. But he is the owner of an enviable record, something Sourav Ganguly would trade all his offside shots for. Srikkanth, or Chikka, returned from the tour of Pakistan in 1989 undefeated as captain. The four Tests played in that series were drawn. The series will be remembered for two things – Srikkanth's poor run of form and the emergence of Sachin Tendulkar, then all of 16. Chikka had a huge role to play in ensuring that Tendulkar's career was not nipped in the bud. Srikkanth was an unlikely candidate for captaincy. When Dilip Vengsarkar pulled out due to personal reasons, the selectors thought it best not to hand the reins back to Kapil Dev or Mohammed Azharuddin, but to this Madras Bomber whose utter disdain for the bowlers is as well known as his famous walk to square-leg after each delivery. He has two centuries against Pakistan, both an identical 123, one in either form of the game.

Batting & Fielding	M	Runs	Avg	H.S.	100	50	S.R.	Ct
ODIs	146	4092	29.02	123	4	27	71.73	42
vs Pakistan	26	688	28.67	123	1	4	73.27	6
Tests	43	2062	29.88	123	2	12	--	40
vs Pakistan	11	436	24.22	123	1	1	--	8

Bowling	M	Wkts	Avg	Best	5WI	S.R.	E.R.
ODIs	146	25	25.64	5/27	2	28.48	5.40
vs Pakistan	26	2	42.00	1/10	--	39.00	6.46
Tests	43	--	--	0/1	--	--	--
vs Pakistan	11	--	--	0/2	--	--	--

Born: **August 31, 1969**
Batting style: **Right-handed**
Bowling style: **Right-arm fast**
Playing years: **1991-2003**

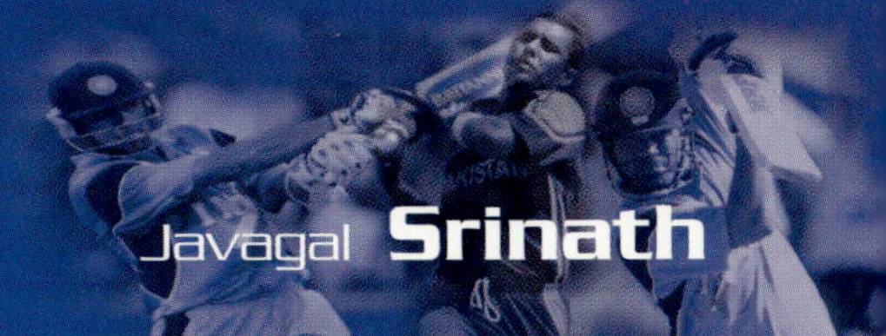

Javagal **Srinath**

Javagal Srinath, the computer engineer from Mysore, just bowled. He preferred to move the ball than to move his lips, a trait which would disqualify him from any modern day fast bowler's club. But that's the way he got most of his sizeable haul of Test and ODI wickets. His most memorable performance came in the Ahmedabad Test match in 1996 against South Africa where he produced an incisive spell of 6 for 21 when the Proteas were chasing a small fourth innings score of 170 and fell short. Sadly, his best effort of 8 for 86 in Test cricket came in a losing cause at Eden Gardens against Pakistan in the Asian Test Championship. Other memorable achievements against Pakistan include his being a part of the team in all the four World Cup wins. Srinath bowling wide of the stumps in the Ferozshah Kotla Test in 1999 when Pakistan were 9 down to enable teammate Anil Kumble to get his record 10-wicket haul is another memory that people will have of this big-hearted cricketer.

Batting & Fielding	M	Runs	Avg	H.S.	100	50	S.R.	Ct
ODIs	229	883	10.64	53	--	1	79.55	32
vs Pakistan	36	177	9.32	43	--	--	85.92	8
Tests	67	1009	14.21	76	--	4	--	22
vs Pakistan	3	66	11.00	49	--	--	--	--

Bowling	M	Wkts	Avg	Best	5WI	S.R.	E.R.
ODIs	229	315	28.09	5/23	3	37.89	4.45
vs Pakistan	36	54	30.69	4/49	--	36.48	5.05
Tests	67	236	30.49	8/86	10	64.00	--
vs Pakistan	3	17	20.65	8/86	2	35.65	--

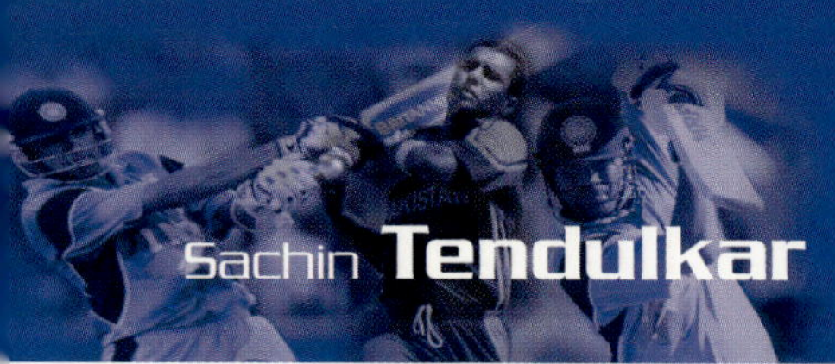

Sachin **Tendulkar**

Till Sachin Tendulkar's wicket falls, no match is termed over. Till he makes the long walk back, the opposition is on tenterhooks. And till his MRF bat is being wielded, India will always be in the hunt. This is not because of the 69 international hundreds he has scored or the 22,355 runs he has plundered at international level. It is just the way he has gone about his cricket ever since he took guard as a 16-year-old at the National Stadium in Karachi on November 15, 1989. If ever there was a player who believed in the maxim 'it is never a wrong time to do the right thing', it is Tendulkar. As a rule he will always attack, as a rule he will always put his best foot forward. Sometimes he will fail, and as a rule, there will be a national debate in India as to whether Tendulkar is out of form. That's the price he has to pay for being the best batsman in the world and a modern day hero in a nation starved of heroes. Many feel his best efforts have come to a lost cause. His 100 against Pakistan in Chennai when he was battling back spasms is now part of folklore and is almost on par with Sunil Gavaskar's 96 against the same opposition on a snake pit in Bangalore in 1987. The painful memories of that knock have been erased by the scorcher he played at Centurion in the 2003 World Cup to help India post their fourth win over Pakistan in the quadrennial event. He showed that the hunger is still there with the 141 he got in Pindi, making him the first Indian to get an ODI 100 in Pakistan.

Batting & Fielding	M	Runs	Avg	H.S.	100	50	S.R.	Ct
ODIs	333	13134	44.83	186*	37	66	86.34	100
vs Pakistan	49	1646	38.28	141	3	10	86.86	25
Tests	112	9459	58.39	241*	33	37	--	72
vs Pakistan	8	589	49.08	194*	2	2	--	2

Bowling	M	Wkts	Avg	Best	5WI	S.R.	E.R.
ODIs	333	116	48.29	5/32	1	57.56	5.03
vs Pakistan	49	15	60.67	3/45	--	68.27	5.33
Tests	112	33	46.06	3/10	--	83.82	--
vs Pakistan	8	6	24.50	2/35	--	40.00	--

Born: **April 24, 1973**
Batting style: **Right-handed**
Bowling style: **Right-arm leg break**
Playing years: **1989-**

Born: **April 6, 1956**
Batting style: **Right-handed**
Bowling style: **Right-arm**
Playing years: **1975-1992**

Dilip Vengsarkar

Along with the alphabets D and V in Dilip Vengsarkar's initials, the letter L would also make a fine companion: L for Lord of Lord's. The elegant right-hander scored three 100s in successive Tests at the Mecca of cricket. Like Rahul Dravid today, the No. 3 slot of the Indian batting order was on his postal address for a long time. The Wisden cricketer of the year award in 1987 probably came when he was at his peak as he scored eight 100s in between 1986 and 1988. Like many subcontinental greats, Vengsarkar raised his game when battling against Pakistan. His Test average against the Old Enemy is two points higher than his career Test average at 44.27 with two 100s and eight 50s. His best feat came at Ferozshah Kotla in the 1979-80 series where he scored 146 not out in the second innings and almost won India the Test that seemed lost. His best ODI innings against Pakistan came in Sialkot in 1984-85. He scored 94 not out and that was the highest score by an Indian in Pakistan in ODIs till Rahul Dravid scored 99 in the opening match at Karachi.

Batting & Fielding	M	Runs	Avg	H.S.	100	50	S.R.	Ct
ODIs	129	3508	34.73	105	1	23	67.81	37
vs Pakistan	25	643	35.72	95*	--	5	63.92	5
Tests	116	6868	42.13	166	17	35	--	78
vs Pakistan	22	1284	44.28	146*	2	8	--	13

Bowling	M	Wkts	Avg	Best	5WI	S.R.	E.R.
ODIs	129	--	--	0/4	--	--	4.00
vs Pakistan	25	Did not bowl					
Tests	116	--	--	0/3	--	--	--
vs Pakistan	22	--	--	0/4	--	--	--

Polly Umrigar

Born: **March 28, 1926**
Batting style: **Right-handed**
Bowling style: **Right-arm medium & off break**
Playing years: **1948-1962**

Umrigar scored the highest number of runs for India in the 60s. He was a right-hand attacking mid-order batsman who could bowl seam-up as well as off-breaks untiringly. He was an outstanding slip fielder with big palms. Above all, he was a good reader of the game whose captaincy ability was not fully used by India. In 59 Tests Umrigar scored 3,631 runs (average 42.22) and took 35 wickets. Umrigar scored a 100 in the Mumbai Test against Pakistan that India won by 10 wickets. He matured on India's first tour of Pakistan. He scored 32 in a low- scoring first Test, claimed 6 for 74 in the second at Bahawalpur, hit 78 in the third at Lahore and 108 in the fourth at Peshawar. In the l960 series against Pakistan, Umrigar rose to the pinnacle scoring hundreds in the Tests at Kanpur, Madras and Delhi. In his playing days, Umrigar was the only one to star in all of India's victories. After retirement he served the game as a selector, national team coach, BCCI executive secretary and ground curator.

Batting & Fielding	M	Runs	Avg	H.S.	100	50	S.R.	Ct
ODIs	Did not play							
vs Pakistan	Did not play							
Tests	59	3631	42.22	223	12	14	--	33
vs Pakistan	15	911	53.59	117	5	2	--	10

Bowling	M	Wkts	Avg	Best	5WI	S.R.	E.R.
ODIs	Did not play						
vs Pakistan	Did not play						
Tests	59	35	42.09	6/74	2	135.00	--
vs Pakistan	15	14	30.36	6/74	1	115.29	--

Born: **November 16, 1971**
Batting style: **Right-handed**
Bowling style: **Right-arm fast**
Playing years: **1989-2004**

Waqar Younis

Waqar Younis was the man who has made the reverse swing a trend and along with Wasim Akram, formed Pakistan's most feared and potent pace attack. He didn't just reverse swing the ball, he also reversed the trend of fast bowlers aiming for the batsman's head or ribs. Instead, Younis aimed at their toes. He got so many of his victims bowled and leg before wicket that one wondered whether he needed the support of the fielders at all. He made his debut in the same Test as Sachin Tendulkar in Karachi 1989 and one of Waqar's great regrets is the fact that he could never bowl to him in Test cricket in his prime, as cricketing ties between India and Pakistan suffered because of political problems. He played quite a few one-dayers against India with his best effort being 5-31 at Sharjah. Sadly for the Pakistani team, Wasim Akram and Waqar Younis were involved in a bitter rivalry later on in their careers and that hurt Pakistan cricket no end. He was made captain in 2001 but after showing promising results early on, he was sacked after Pakistan's disastrous World Cup campaign.

Batting & Fielding	M	Runs	Avg	H.S.	100	50	S.R.	Ct
ODIs	262	969	10.31	37	--	--	67.34	35
vs India	26	67	22.33	13*	-	--	70.53	3
Tests	87	1010	10.20	45	--	--	--	18
vs India	4	16	5/33	6*	--	--	--	1

Bowling	M	Wkts	Avg	Best	5WI	S.R.	E.R.
ODIs	262	416	23.84	7/36	13	30.52	4.69
vs India	26	37	24.49	5/31	1	31.78	4.62
Tests	87	373	23.56	7/76	22	43.50	--
vs India	4	8	48.75	4/80	--	80.25	--

Born: **July 24, 1947**

Batting style: **Right-handed**

Bowling style: **Right-arm**

Playing years: **1969-1985**

Zaheer Abbas

Zaheer ab bas (Zaheer, that's enough)! That is what the Indians were exclaiming each time they toured Pakistan in 1978, 1982-83 and 1984-85. Zaheer had a penchant for Indian bowling, but only on Pakistani wickets. He was a major success in home series but when it came to scoring in India, Zaheer was a big disappointment. That would eternally remain a puzzle. Zaheer had just 313 runs while playing in India with just one half-century. On the other hand, he took apart the Indian bowlers in Pakistan, notching up 1427 runs in 11 Tests with six centuries. A stylish batsman and a handsome man, Zaheer was amongst the fortunate to lead Pakistan against India. Zaheer would have preferred to get it by right, but a shin injury to Imran Khan saw Zaheer being appointed as captain by default. His appetite for runs was such that Zaheer was termed the Asian Bradman. During the 1989 series, Mohammed Azharuddin approached Zaheer who made minor alterations in Azhar's grip. Azhar relaunched his career with a magnificent 109 in the second Test at Faisalabad.

Batting & Fielding	M	Runs	Avg	H.S.	100	50	S.R.	Ct
ODIs	62	2572	47.63	123	7	13	84.86	15
vs India	13	612	51.00	118	3	1	97.14	2
Tests	78	5062	44.80	274	12	20	--	34
vs India	19	1740	87.00	235*	6	3	--	6

Bowling	M	Wkts	Avg	Best	5WI	S.R.	E.R.
ODIs	62	7	31.86	2/26	--	40.00	4.78
vs India	13	2	19.50	2/33	--	15.00	7.80
Tests	78	3	44.00	2/21	--	123.33	--
vs India	19	1	41.00	1/14	--	96.00	--

TEAM OF CONTRIBUTORS

Omar Kureishi

Omar Kureishi was born in Murree, of a Punjabi father and a Kashmiri mother. He grew up in pre-Partition India, in New Delhi, Pune and Mumbai where he went to Cathedral High School and Ismail Yousouf College, going on to study further at the University of Southern California.

The author of seven books – 'some political, some autobiographical but none on cricket' – he is one of Pakistan's best-known cricket commentators, and continues to write a column on cricket, as well as one on politics, for the national daily, *Dawn*. Earlier, he was News Editor of *The Pakistan Standard*, and Editor of *The Times of Karachi*. He was also Director of Public Affairs of Pakistan International Airlines.

He was awarded the Sitara-I-Imtiaz, one of Pakistan's highest civil honours. He lives in Karachi.

Rajdeep Sardesai

One of the best-known faces on the small screen, Rajdeep Sardesai joined New Delhi Television (NDTV) in 1994 after a six-year innings with *The Times of India*. He is now Managing Editor & Political Editor of NDTV, and hosts two of its most popular weekly shows, 'The Big Fight' and 'Ex Factor'. He is also currently doing two election specials, 'Election Watch' and 'The Live Election Programme'.

Though the media is his profession, cricket is his passion – not surprisingly for the son of one of the ace cricketers of yesteryears, Dilip Sardesai. While his viewers may be more accustomed to seeing him engage in combat with his interviewees on screen, Sardesai Jr. is no mean cricketer himself, having captained his school team in Mumbai and played first class cricket at Oxford.

Ayaz Memon

His love of the game has translated into 25 years of writing on cricket. Veteran journalist and sports writer Ayaz Memon has covered five World Cups, and has followed Indo-Pak cricket from 1982, when he crossed the Wagah border to get a ringside view of the match between India and its neighbour, till the present series. Formerly editor of *Sportsweek*, he has also covered the 1988 Olympics, the 1990 Asian Games and the 1998 Commonwealth Games. From 1993 until 2000, he was editor of *Mid-day* in Mumbai. He is currently National Sports Editor and Editor, Bombay Times, of *The Times of India*, Mumbai.

Madhu Trehan

Madhu Trehan's name will always be associated with India's most successful news magazine, *India Today*, though her brother Aroon Purie now runs it. Trehan started the magazine more than 30 years ago, before moving to New York, where she lived for 20 years with her doctor husband, Naresh Trehan, and two daughters. On her return to India in 1989, she started Newstrack, a video news magazine that proved to be a pathbreaker in pioneering TV journalism. She was involved in the creation of Aaj Tak, the Hindi news channel of TV Today, but left to start a website, wahindia.com, at the height of the dotcom boom. Since its closure, she is busy writing a book on Tehelka to be published by Roli Books, and asserts that 'at my age, this is exactly where I want to be.'

Nina Martyris

Having grown up in India's steel city, Jamshedpur, Nina Martyris began her career in journalism in 1995 with *The Times of India,* Mumbai, where she is now Special Correspondent. Her normal beat is lifestyle and the city of Mumbai. The 2004 Indo-Pak series led to the discovery of two new loves – cricket, and the people of Pakistan.

Kadambari Murali

Currently Special Correspondent with the *Hindustan Times* in New Delhi, Kadambari Murali began her career in journalism with *The Pioneer* in 1996, after graduating in Political Science from Hindu College, Delhi University. Prior to joining the *Hindustan Times*, she worked with the *Indian Express* and the *Asian Age*. Murali covered the just-concluded Indo-Pak cricket series together with her husband, Kunal Pradhan, a sports correspondent with Reuters.

Rajesh Kumar

An internationally-known cricket statistician, Rajesh Kumar has been contributing regularly for several years to publications in India and abroad, including the 'cricketing Bible', the *Wisden Cricketers' Almanac*, the *ACS International Cricket Yearbook*, UK, the *Playfair Cricket Annual,* the journal of the Cricket Society of England, and *The Cricketer International Quarterly*.

Apart from assisting Bill Frindall, a leading international cricket statistician, Kumar is also the cricket statistician for NDTV, *The Times of India*, and several websites.

Sunil Warrier is Sports-in-Charge, Junior Assistant Editor, *The Times of India,* Mumbai

Pradeep Vijaykar is Assistant Editor, *The Times of India,* Mumbai

Nitin Naik is Copy Editor-cum-Correspondent, *The Times of India,* Mumbai

Anant Gaundalkar is Statistician, *The Times of India,* Mumbai

Pradeep Mandhani

No cricket match would be complete without his camera. Since 1982, when he began his career in cricket photography with *The Sunday Mail,* Pradeep Mandhani has covered more than 1000 one-day internationals and 120 Test matches around the globe, the most recent being the just-concluded Indo-Pak series. Mandhani's photographs appear regularly in leading newspapers and sports journals in India and abroad. He has published several books of his photographs, including *Independence Cup, My World Cup, ESPN Star Sports World Cup Frozen '99,* and *ESPN Star Sports World Cup Frozen '94.* His pictures have also appeared in Kapil Dev's *Triumph of the Spirit* and the late Mark Mascarenhas' books on the Independence Cup and the World Cup.

Pradeep Mandhani's picture of Jonty Rhodes won him the Fujifilm Best Picture Award in the World Cup 1996, while he was honoured by Canon as Best Sports Photographer of India in 1998.

Acknowledgements

The Publishers would like to express their gratitude to Zubeida Mustafa, *The Dawn*, Ameena Sayyid, Oxford University Press, Pakistan, and Shoaib Ahmed, Pakistan, for their help and support in sourcing pictures and material at short notice.

ISBN: 81-7436-320-3

Editors: Renuka Chatterjee, Nandita Jaishankar
Design: Sneha Pamneja
Production: Kumar Raman, Narendar Shahi, Naresh Nigam

Published in India by Roli Books
M-75 Greater Kailash-II (Market)
New Delhi 110 048, India.
Phone: ++91-11-29212271, 29212782
Fax: ++91-11-29217185
Email: roli@vsnl.com
Website: rolibooks.com

Printed and bound in India